Recovery from Abusive Groups

Wendy Ford

American Family Foundation

An American Family Foundation Book

Recovery from Abusive Groups

About the Author

Wendy Ford was recruited into a Bible-based cult in 1973 while a freshman at college. She was in the cult for seven years. While involved, she completed two intensive leadership indoctrination programs, a survival program which included shooting firearms and hitchhiking alone, and traveled throughout the United States. On May 16, 1980, after one failed deprogramming the previous Fall, she was successfully deprogrammed by her parents. After returning home, she completed her B.A. at Harvard University while working.

Ms. Ford has counseled many ex-cultists, their families, and friends. She has been interviewed extensively on cults both by the media and the government. She has appeared on local and national television and has lectured to many groups, including high school, college, law enforcement, and religious audiences. From 1987 to 1990 she was the New England Director for FOCUS, an ex-cultist support group and is presently a Research Associate with the American Family Foundation.

After several years in electronic publishing, Ms. Ford is in the process of changing careers. She is attending graduate school for a Masters in Education and for state certification as a middle school social studies teacher, both to be completed in June of 1994. She is also involved with a women's group, local Unitarian Universalist parish, and sings jazz. She lives with her fiancé in a Boston suburb.

American Family Foundation
P.O. Box 2265
Bonita Springs, FL 33959.

This book is a revised, second edition of *Some Thoughts on Recovery*, copyright © 1990, Wendy Ford.

Cover graphic by Jennifer Powell.

Intended Audience

This handbook was written for people who have been traumatized by abusive groups, in particular cults. This handbook is also helpful for those who have been hurt by someone else's involvement in an abusive group. Cults are characterized as closed groups that use extreme psychological manipulation (abuse) to exploit people. Chapter Four is written specifically to the friends and family of someone in recovery.

If you were not in an abusive group, or are close to someone who was/is in an abusive group, you may still find in these pages ideas that can help you. Many who read the first edition and who came from abusive relationships, alcoholic families, or other all-consuming situations, have found this book very encouraging and helpful.

Library of Congress Catalog Card No: 93-071153

ISBN 0-931337-04-6

Printed in the United States of America

10 9 8 7 6 5 4 3 2 1

Table of Contents

Exercises

Acknowledgments

It would be difficult to thank all the many people who have helped me over the years to recover from this very painful and disorienting experience. Family, friends, therapists, coworkers, CAN and AFF have helped me to heal and grow. I am very grateful to them all.

I would like to extend a special thank you to the Boston FOCUS group. They have been a wonderful example to me of how ex-cultists can grow and heal through courage, determination, and compassion for one other. I have learned so much from them. Without them, this handbook would still be on the back burner.

Thank you, also, to all the many people who have made suggestions on how to improve this handbook. You will find many of your suggestions in this second edition.

Thank you all!

What You Can Do to Help

Everyone connected in anyway to the ex-cultist can be helpful, even the brief encounter at a party or on a bus ride can be supportive. You can be supportive by listening to and sympathizing with the ex-cultist without judgment and without the offering of unsolicited opinions, such as "I never would have listened to them." (See Chapter Four.)

Most ex-cultists and their families do not get enough good information about what abusive groups are, how they work, and how to recover from the experience. There is so much more information available these days, so point them to their local library and bookstore. The Cult Awareness Network (CAN) also carries many good books and has information packages available for a small donation. For information write to CAN, 2421 West Pratt Boulevard, Suite 1173, Chicago, IL 60645, phone 312-267-7777.

You can also contact the American Family Foundation (AFF) for information by writing AFF at P.O. Box 2265, Bonita Springs, FL 33959-2265, phone 212-249-7693. The American Family Foundation publishes reports and books that give advice to families and helping professionals. AFF also publishes a scholarly journal on cults. Many of their excellent articles are referenced in the Reference List at the end of this handbook. Both CAN and AFF also produce regular newsletters that are available for a small donation.

Ex-members may want to consider a subscription to FOCUS News. FOCUS is a national support group for ex-cultists. For information write: FOCUS News, c/o CAN National Office, 2421 West Pratt Boulevard, Suite 1173, Chicago, IL 60645.

For additional excellent information, please review the Recommended Reading and Additional Readings lists in the back of this handbook. You may also want to review the reading lists in both Steve Hassan's (1988) book and Carol Giambalvo's (1991) book. Their lists are excellent.

Preface

Until recently, the area of cultic study which has received the least amount of attention has been that of the post-cult period. Focus has been placed upon defining modern day destructive cults, delineating the ways they approach people, and describing the manipulation and techniques used by cults to achieve an altered state of consciousness. Most autobiographical accounts of cult life have emphasized the pre-cult period, the recruitment phase, cult life, intervention, and reassessment of commitment to the cult. Usually, only a short epilogue addresses the recovery process. Recognizing the need for more emphasis on the recovery phase, the American Family Foundation in 1989 launched Project Recovery which brought together groups of experts to study specific aspects of the cult phenomenon. Their findings will appear in a book entitled *Recovery from Cults*, edited by Dr. Michael Langone and scheduled to be published in September 1993.

Researchers have also begun to conduct ongoing studies of the recovery process of former cultists. Most notably, Dr. Paul Martin, in collaboration with Dr. Langone and others, has been studying post-cult distress and treatment modalities which have been adopted to help ameliorate this distress.

Another example of the response to the need for literature on the recovery process is the book which you now hold. Wendy Ford has written an honest, revealing, highly comprehensive and practical guide for former cultists and their families. We have had the pleasure of knowing Wendy for the last twelve years, since she exited from her cult. At American Family Foundation and Cult Awareness Network conferences, she has informally and generously been available to help others, serving as a guide to recently exited members and their families. Over the years, we have found her observations to be valuable and her warm engaging personality to be delightful. Fortunately for the reader, Wendy's intelligent and thoughtful approach to helping others is captured on the pages of this book.

Instead of simply listing issues which confront former cultists and their families, Wendy offers the reader practical suggestions for dealing with each of these issues. In this second edition, she extends this resourceful book into a workbook by asking thought-provoking questions entitled "Exercises" at the end of each section. This approach can be particularly helpful to former cultists who have been induced to be passive recipients of information through destructive cult techniques. Wendy encourages the reader to actively participate in the recovery process. She also is candid about her personal struggles in leaving her cult. We are confident that the reader will see herself or himself in Wendy's struggles.

Each of the issues discussed in this book has been faced by former cultists whom we have seen in therapy. In fact, seventeen years ago we decided to begin a support group for former cultists for the purpose of helping them realize that they are not alone in their post-cult struggles. By dealing with these struggles in a book format, former cultists, particularly those who are isolated from other exited cult members, will see how universal the post-cult aftereffects are. Naturally, the reader will not be able to identify with every issue. However, we have no doubt that each reader will find issues which will relate to him or her.

Former cultists report feeling isolated and confused by their cult experiences. Few family members and friends understand all that they have been through. Many former cultists report attempting to suppress their post-cult difficulties for many years until it becomes clear that the experience of having been in an abusive group continues to limit their present life in numerous ways. Wendy is able to convey to the reader an understanding of the harmful impact of cult life based upon her own experience and the experiences of the families she has worked with over the years. Wendy has been a resource of knowledge. Through this sensible, instructive book, a wider circle of people will now have the opportunity to benefit from her wise and practical step-by-step approach. This book is the first of its kind, and it will be difficult to surpass.

Lorna Goldberg, M.S.W., A.C.S.W.
William Goldberg, M.S.W., A.C.S.W.
Englewood, New Jersey

Introduction

But screw your courage to the sticking place,
And we'll not fail.
          - Macbeth

In 1980 I left The Way International, one of the most successful cults of the 1970s. For more than ten years I have struggled to rebuild my life. From those struggles has come a great deal of learning, growth, and healing. I thought I would share with you my thoughts on the process, what has and hasn't worked for me, in the hope that your healing or the healing of one you hold dear will be less painful and less time-consuming.

You may find in these pages ideas that can help you even if you were not in a cult but were in another abusive or all-consuming relationship. Many who have read the first edition and who came from abusive relationships, such as alcoholic spouses or families, have commented that they found this book very helpful and encouraging.

Ingredients for Recovery

I have learned that there are three main ingredients needed for recovery. Without these, you can only heal a little bit. They are:

1. Time
2. Discipline
3. Courage

It took a great deal of time to heal, much more time than I ever imagined. It took a tremendous amount of mental discipline to disassemble the tangled web of the group's "logic." As I recovered from this snare, I was disheartened to find embedded in our culture additional "logic" also of dubious nature, and so my work to disassemble did not and could not end with the group. And, it took courage. Courage to face a depth of hopelessness I pray I never face again. Courage to let go of myths and wishes and fantasies, and to let go of innocence.

Working it Out

This book pulls together what I've learned helping ex-cultists and their families since 1980, but I am not a trained counselor or psychiatrist. This book is not intended to and should not replace good therapeutic and medical help. Many, many people have expressed to me how very helpful this book has been. I think you will find some good ideas and suggestions here. As you read it through and discuss the ideas and exercises with family and friends, pick out what you think will work for you. These are suggestions, not a "bible."

What is a Destructive Group?

Below are listed the marks and techniques of a destructive group as noted in the Cult Awareness Network's brochure. For an in-depth reading on the psychological steps and techniques of coercion, see Lifton's classic work entitled *Thought Reform and the Psychology of Totalism* (1961), specifically Chapters 5, 12 and 22. (See Appendices B and C.)

Marks of a Destructive Group

The marks of a destructive group are as follows:

1. **Mind Control** (undue influence): manipulation by use of coercive persuasion or behavior modification techniques without informed consent.

2. **Charismatic Leadership**: claiming divinity or special knowledge and demanding unquestioning obedience with power and privilege. Leadership may consist of one individual or a small core of leaders.

3. **Deception**: recruiting and fundraising with hidden objectives and without full disclosure of the use of mind controlling techniques [group psychology]; use of "front groups."

4. **Exclusivity**: secretiveness or vagueness by followers regarding activities and beliefs.

5. **Alienation**: separation from family, friends, and society, a change in values and substitution of the cult as the new "family," evidence of subtle or abrupt personality changes.

6. **Exploitation**: can be financial, physical, or psychological; pressure to give money, to spend a great deal on courses or give excessively to special projects and to engage in inappropriate sexual activities, even child abuse.

7. **Totalitarian Worldview** (we/they syndrome): effecting dependence, promoting goals of the group over the individual and approving unethical behavior while claiming goodness.

Techniques of a Destructive Group

The techniques of a destructive group are as follows:

1. **Group Pressure** and **"Love-Bombing"** discourages doubts and reinforces the need to belong through use of child-like games, singing, hugging, touching, or flattery.

2. **Isolation/Separation** causes an inability or lack of desire to verify the reality of information provided by the group.

3. **Thought-Stopping Techniques** introduce recruits to meditating, chanting, and repetitious activities which, when used excessively, induce a state of high suggestibility.

4. **Fear and Guilt** induced by eliciting confessions to produce intimacy and to reveal fears and secrets, by creating emotional vulnerability through overt and covert threats, and by alternating punishment and reward.

5. **Sleep Deprivation** encouraged under the guise of spiritual exercises, necessary training, or urgent projects.

6. **Inadequate Nutrition** sometimes disguised as a special diet to improve health or advance spirituality, or as rituals requiring fasting.

7. **Sensory Overload** forces acceptance of complex new doctrines, goals, and definitions to replace old values by expecting recruit to assimilate masses of information quickly with little opportunity for critical examination.

Not all of these techniques need to be present simultaneously for a mind control environment to be operative.

Harmful Effects of a Destructive Group

The harmful effects of a destructive group may include:

1. Loss of free will and control over one's life.

2. Development of dependency and return to child-like behavior.

3. Loss of spontaneity or sense of humor.

4. Inability to form intimate friendships outside the cult or enjoy flexible relationships.

5. Physical deterioration and abuse.

6. Psychological deterioration (including hallucinations, anxiety, paranoia, disorientation, and dissociation).

7. Involuntary, *de facto* servitude or exploitation.

Not all of these harmful effects will be experienced by everyone who has a destructive group experience.

Structure of this Handbook

This handbook consists of an introduction, four chapters, and appendices. Within each chapter are a number of topics that address different feelings and issues for that phase of recovery. The topics are organized somewhat chronologically. Exercises are presented to help stimulate thinking about how the topic being discussed affects the reader. These are completely optional and are presented here simply as learning aids. The appendices provide additional information, including study questions and a recommended reading list.

Buzz Words and Hot Buttons

I have tried not to use phrasing that might remind readers of their cult lingo ("loaded language"). Because there are at least several thousand cults, which are changing and mutating constantly, it is impossible for me to avoid touching off some buttons for some people. I am sorry about this. I have tried not to use loaded words. If some of the phrasing I've used touches hot spots for you, you may want to try using this problem as a chance to dismantle the cues. If you should start floating or if you should feel shaky while reading any part of this handbook, ask someone to talk with you about what you are experiencing. (See Floating, p. 36.)

Factors in Recovery

Since 1980 I have talked with many ex-cultists, their families, friends, spouses, and acquaintances in an informal counseling and supportive role not only as an ex-cultist but from 1987 to 1990 as the New England Regional Director for FOCUS, a national support group for ex-cultists. From these many conversations and from my own experiences, it seems to me that a number of factors affect a person's ability to recover and the rate of recovery:

- How emotionally developed and psychologically healthy the person was before being recruited
- How severe the split was between the former self and the cult self
- Types of experiences within the cult, such as sexual, nutritional, physical, emotional, psychic, and ritual abuse
- Type and quality of exit, whether:
    - Kicked out
    - Forced deprogramming intervention
    - Non-forced exit counseling intervention
    - Walkaway
- Support of other ex-cultists, especially those from the same group
- Support and acceptance by family and friends
- Professional help received after exiting, such as:
    - Individual and group counseling
    - Residential recovery facility, i.e. "rehab"

- Medical attention
- State social services
- Legal services, particularly child custody
- Career and job placement services
- Time to heal and work through issues before taking on any major commitments, such as school and/or career
- Mental discipline to reclaim (or develop) critical thinking faculties, even when doing so gets difficult
- Courage to face the pain of loss and to stick with the process of grieving even when it gets painful

Phases in Recovery

The recovery process can span any length of time and, basically, breaks out into three main phases. These three phases are:

1. Awareness and Exit
2. Understanding and Feeling
3. Rebuilding and Dreaming

Phase One – Awareness and Exit

This first phase varies in length, and is often dependent on the method of exiting. This phase is marked by the experiences that alert members to the danger of the group and result in the member's exiting permanently.

The key to an effective exit is to "jump start" the critical thinking process of the mind. This process has been on hold for much too long because the group has told the followers that to question and doubt the group is to betray God (or whatever). The price for questioning and doubting, they are told, is eternal death. This is a very powerful fear to overcome.

Awareness of the insidious nature of the cult and the decision to leave comes slowly for some and quickly for others. For example, someone forcibly deprogrammed becomes aware and leaves the cult very quickly as compared to someone who walks out after reflecting over several months or years on "devil-inspired" doubts.

Even after leaving, some ex-cultists are not sure if they made the right decision and "float" in between their old cult identity and their new liberated identity or pre-cult self. (See Floating, p. 36.) The more information and support cultists receives during this phase, the better equipped they are to handle the pain and loss of Phase Two.

Phase Two – Understanding and Feeling

The second phase is full of ups and downs, of feeling as if you just returned from Mars, of exciting new freedoms and discoveries, and it is also full of rage and pain. It involves coming to terms with being raped, emotionally and spiritually. And for many, it involves coming to terms with being physically raped as well.

I don't know how to convey the extremes of pain possible in this phase. Perhaps it is how you would feel standing by helplessly as some crazy person slowly murdered someone you loved. It seems so incredible to many that because they wanted to serve God and their country, wanted to help people, and wanted to make the world a better place—for this idealism (or selflessness) they were cruelly used. This is a very difficult aspect of the experience to reconcile. "What ever did I do to be treated like this?" is a question that rings deep in the heart of any ex-cultist. The answer to this question resides in understanding how mind control techniques work.

It is no wonder, then, that the rage and anger the ex-cultist feels is often overwhelming and frightening. So much so, that many tend to repress or deny the full expression of their emotions. But understanding and feeling one's emotions in a nondestructive way, I believe, is critical to recovery.

This second phase can be an extraordinary journey through pain and loss to learning and mastery. It varies in length and is dependent on how able the ex-cultist is to experience loss and how disciplined the ex-cultist is to study, think, and work toward a thorough understanding of the experience.

Learning to Trust Again

One of the truly tough parts about working through the experience is the very fact that it's a very big job. The ex-cultist must learn how to trust life again, and learning to trust requires learning how to test reality. Because the cult phobias and teachings often touched on many aspects of life, such as family, government, education, religion, relationships, and economics, the ex-cultist often finds it necessary to examine and reality test most, if not all, of the teachings received in the cult for subtle, residual ideas that continue to manipulate the ex-cultist.

In addition, it is in this phase that individuals must learn again how to trust themselves and their ability to make decisions. Learning to trust after you have been used and hurt can be very scary, but trust in yourself and in others can be rebuilt with disciplined thinking and courage.

For those who come from dysfunctional backgrounds, recovering from the cult experience often means acknowledging and recovering from the effects of earlier patterns (Black, 1982), such as:

- Abusive parents, relatives, siblings, spouse
- Behaving abusively toward others
- Alcoholism, rape, incest, eating disorders, drug abuse
- Difficulties with intimacy, careers, law enforcement

If ex-cultists are willing to "roll up their sleeves" and "dig their heels in," and to work through and out of the past, then they can move onto Phase Three, that of rebuilding one's life and building toward a dream.

Phase Three – Rebuilding and Dreaming

To someone in the middle of the pain of Phase Two, the idea of having a dream again and building toward it is merely a sad, frustrating, and painful laugh. Having spent many years in Phase Two, I understand that despondent feeling very well.

It is possible to rebuild your life. You will not be able to make up for all the years the cult has stolen from you, but you can make up for some of those lost years. I've worked very hard to recover from an overprotective and domineering family, seven years in a cult, a rape while in the cult, two forced deprogrammings each with conservatorships, a lawsuit for trying to help someone out of a cult, too many job changes, and too many unfulfilling relationships after the cult.

If you are willing to stick with it, to work at it, to work through and let go of myths that look like truths, not only in the cult but also in society, and if you are willing to acquire new skills and improve others, you can build a healthy and well-functioning life with a dream you can work toward.

Chapter 1:
Phase One–Awareness and Exit

*The past is but the beginning of a beginning, and all
that is and has been is but the twilight of the dawn.*
—H. G. Wells

For me, awareness came in the form of one tall, good-looking West
Virginian, who stopped me on the sidewalk as I was on my way to work.
It seemed a bit odd to me that he was asking for directions to a bar at
5:30 in the morning that chilly May day in 1980, but he was. I didn't
notice the parked car next to him. When it dawned on me that he was
going to try and kidnap me to have me deprogrammed, I started to run.
But he, thank God, was quicker than I, and he shoved me into the back
seat of the car.

Before I knew it, my father had jumped into the front seat. This time, he
assured me in his most no-nonsense, former collegiate wrestler tone,
there would be no slip-ups, unlike the last deprogramming attempt six
months earlier. During that deprogramming, I escaped out of the New
York motel where I was being held and headed back to the cult in
Michigan as I had been programmed to do. Not this time, though. This
time I was driven from Michigan to West Virginia and there confronted
with a lot of information about the cult I didn't even know existed.

There was a lot of talking, sleeping, and some crying as the reality of
what I had been entrapped in slowly crept over me. I was finally in an
environment which allowed me and encouraged me to talk about the
doubts and contradictions I had been programmed to bury within me.
After a few days of deprogramming, the spell was broken. I then began
the strangest journey I'm sure I'll ever know.

Walkaways

Some people are not deprogrammed as I was. For some the awareness
that the group they are in has unacceptable qualities, and the desire to
exit come differently. Many walk out of the situation or are cast out,
while some emerge from the group over time as the control techniques
falter.

Walkaways and castaways often have serious adjustment problems for
years, because they have not left the group conceptually. The body is not
there, but the mind is still influenced by residual controls and phobias.

While they were still active with a group, it may have been a conversation with someone, a letter from home, an abuse within the cult that started them wondering if something was wrong. Somehow, something cracks through the information control at a point when the individual is vulnerable and it raises a doubt that can no longer be repressed, a gnawing feeling that something is very wrong. That doubt, when nurtured, starts to make some "thinking space." This is why I suggest to family and friends to use any situation with the cultist to create a crack while avoiding direct confrontation. Interject some piece of information that requires reflection and evaluation.

This might include:

- Reaffirmation of love and care
- Stimulating a favorable memory
- Asking a question about the cult that cannot be answered yes or no

Thinking is to the brain what exercise is to the body, and thinking is what starts to open a crack in the cultist's closed mind.

Ex-cultists, who have had a formal intervention, often think that walkaways have it a little easier in recovery because walkaways do not have the trauma of the intervention process. Many walkaways will tell you, though, that the price they have paid is one of extra lost years. Also, most of the thousands of walkaways do not receive any exit counseling, often because they do not realize they have been in a cult. They often wrestle for years with this major life trauma without the appropriate help or guidance as to how the problems they are facing may be cult-related.

Interventions

Until recent years, many ex-cultists were helped out of the clutches of these insidious groups through forced deprogrammings or through non-forced exit counselings. I did not appreciate the significant difference between these two intervention methods until I stumbled into the realization that much of the fear and anxiety I was experiencing as an ex-cultist (now known as Post Traumatic Stress Syndrome) was due to the method of intervention—two forced deprogrammings each with a conservatorship.

A conservatorship is a legal document which gave my parents legal guardianship of me even though I was an adult. My parents took this measure to protect themselves. If the deprogramming did not work and I returned to the cult and was "encouraged" to sue them as many cultists have been instructed to do by their cult leaders, my parents could have lost everything they owned. A conservatorship is harder to get today than it was ten years ago.

Let me explain a little about these two very different methods of intervention (See Clark, Giambalvo, Giambalvo, Garvey, & Langone, 1993; and Giambalvo, 1992).

Deprogramming

Forced deprogrammings involve the use of security personnel to abduct and hold cultists against their will while a confrontational discussion takes place usually over several days. Conservatorship papers may or may not have been granted. This type of intervention can be traumatic and, when performed on an adult, may be declared illegal if charges are brought.

What makes this type of intervention so traumatic is that the loved one loses all relationships with the cult instantaneously. Though this is often of great relief to family and friends, it is an immediate and, therefore, traumatic sense of loss for the individual, unlike the walkaway who has separated over time. It is my opinion that this method of intervention should be used only after great deliberation and as a last resort. Those who choose it should realize that they may have to defend their decision in court. See Langone and Martin (1993) for a discussion of the ethics of deprogramming.

Even when handled smoothly by a well-trained deprogrammer, this type of "radical surgery" may cause scars and anxieties. Some families may have no other choice, since most cultists are taught to flee any type of confrontation about their involvement in the group. In addition, some cults teach their followers to attack, escape, tune out, or commit suicide if confronted by a "disbeliever" in a secured environment.

Exit Counseling

This intervention method is different from deprogramming in one very critical way—individuals are not held against their will. Therefore, it is not illegal. It is also not as traumatic for the individual. Cultists can leave if they choose and are, therefore, more empowered than cultists in a forced deprogramming. Empowerment can help to minimize the trauma of the intervention process (Hassan, 1988).

This intervention method requires more interpersonal skill on the part of the counselor. It also requires more upfront work with the family, preparing them for their role in the intervention and the recovery.

Preparing the family can be very hard to do. Families often see the intervention as the key part of the recovery process. But the work that follows the intervention is the critical part of recovery. "Just get Whoever out of that group so they can go on with their life." Exiting the cult is only the *beginning* of the work, not the end of it.

The main goal in working with family (and sometimes friends) is to build a well-informed, healthy, support system that can help cultists during the intervention as well as when they return home and start rebuilding their lives. Given that some ex-cultists were in their groups 5–20 years, rebuilding their lives after the intervention becomes a very significant issue.

Counseling the family before the intervention also helps to identify family problems. All families have some problems. In order to build the healthiest support system possible, these problems should be identified and addressed prior to the intervention.

Working with the family not only takes well-developed interpersonal skills, it takes time. Time costs money. Some families cannot or will not spend the time and the money. (Ironically, deprogramming usually costs much more because of the security needs.) Minimal preparation both psychologically and informationally can jeopardize this type of intervention and often does. But when this process is done correctly by family and counselor alike, it is much more respectful of the individual and less intrusive or traumatic.

I believe that exit counselors should be certified in some way. It will take some work to establish the criteria for such certification, but it can be done. Establishing a certification procedure and review board would also be a great example to ex-cultists of how responsible professionals hold themselves and their colleagues accountable.

Exercise–Leaving the Group

Write down the answers to the following questions: How did you leave your group? What was it that you saw or learned that helped you leave? Try writing down in chronological order the story of how and why you left. This process will help you focus, stimulate critical thinking, and will provide a handy reminder should your resolve get a little shaky.

I found all this exiting business to be very traumatic, embarrassing, and terribly painful. The residual phobias and anxieties it left were frightening and exhausting. The most helpful words I heard during the intervention were "being in the group was not your fault; you were tricked." These words were reinforced by my family and these words helped me not to get bogged down in guilt and shame.

Phobias

An intervention may leave phobias. A phobia is an intense, illogical, or abnormal fear. These phobias can last for years unless they are "weeded" out through the mental discipline of reality testing. Phobias need to be tested and thereby disproved (See Hassan, 1988).

I had a phobia of vans for a few years. Because I was onced raped in a car and because I was picked up off the street and shoved into a car by the deprogrammers, I had a terror of walking past standing cars or vans for a few years afterwards, until I got more mentally disciplined about testing the phobia. This fear also decreased once I got my own car and did not have to walk to wherever I was going.

Once on a business trip, I was being driven from the airport to my destination. The driver got lost. I had such an extreme panic attack that I almost jumped out of a fast-moving car. My mind was a cloud of panic. All I could do was to keep repeating over and over to myself "I'm in control of my life; I'm in control of my life." Thank goodness, it worked.

Building a Recovery Plan

When athletes are hurt, coaches often design a recovery plan. I suggest ex-cultists do the same thing. There has usually been a lot of damage done to the body, emotions, mind, and spirit. My father once remarked to my brother, who couldn't understand why I wasn't "getting on with my life" after several months of recovery, that Wendy had been hit by a kind of Mack truck. "You just wouldn't expect her to get up and start running again in a short while." It was going to take time; and it was going to take help from others. As I mentioned earlier, healing these wounds takes time, discipline, and courage. A plan can help provide a framework and a focus to this healing process. How do you build a plan?

What's Needed for a Successful Recovery?

You can figure out what you will need by:

- Talking with other ex-cultists
- Reading about recovering from abusive groups and trauma
- Thinking about what you want for the future
- Talking with counseling professionals, for example psychologists, social workers, psychiatrists

Write down ideas and suggestions that seem helpful to you about how to proceed in your recovery (See Stoner and Kisser, 1992; Tobias, 1993) . Try to arrange these ideas into some type of timeline, order or structure.

Group the ideas and suggestions into priorities—most important to least important. For example, if you do not have a place to live, finding housing will be the highest priority. If you want to pick up playing the piano again to reconnect with your past, and also need to find child care so you can work, then playing the piano is a lesser priority. If this all seems too overwhelming for you right now skip this section. Don't push yourself.

Exercise-Assessment

Try asking yourself the following questions and writing down the anwers:

1. *What are my immediate priorities? For example, healthcare, housing, finances, emotional support.*
2. *What are my priorities for the next 3 months? 6 months? year? 2 years? For example, contacting ex-cultists, studying mind control techniques, getting counseling, finding reliable and affordable day care, legal assistance.*
3. *What can I do by myself and what requires the help of others?*
4. *Ask yourself: Who can help me? What do I need to do? When should I do this? Where can I do this? Why am I doing this? How will I do this?*

Other Sources of Help

Some ex-cultists may spend one to several weeks in a residential rehab facility that specializes in cult issues. Other ex-cultists study, go to ex-cult or trauma support groups, get counseling, write, draw, or dance.

Some make career goals, which may involve going back to school. Some need housing, day care, legal assistance, and medical attention. Almost all need thorough medical, dental, and eye exams. Most need lots of sleep, good nutrition, and moderate regular exercise. And all need to talk out their experiences with family, friends, and/or a therapist. There are many good books on the above topics. Check out your libraries, bookstores, and even the phone directory, which often list help centers in your area.

The real work of recovery is not to "get on with things" or to go back into the cult and save others, but, most importantly, it is to go through the work and pain of integrating the experience into a whole and more healthy you. This won't just happen, like some mystical revelation. It's going to take work and planning by you.

Where are You Going to Live?

If, like me, you had no money after exiting the cult, you may have gone (or will go) to where a family member lives. Painfully, you may have had to leave your loved ones and possessions behind in order to get free.

Those exiting with dependents of their own, children and/or elderly parents, may have additional difficulty in locating affordable housing. Also, without a job history, it can be difficult to find work and pay living expenses. With all the emotional difficulties of recovery, even if you find a job it may be tough to keep it once the numbness wears off and depression sets in.

I do not have a quick and easy answer to this problem. You can contact your state agency for housing and ask for help. There may be a friend, coworker, or relative who can help out. Perhaps you could get a scholarship and go back to school.

No Hidden Agendas

If you have a choice of where to live, live with someone who will encourage you to make your own decisions. If you come from a family that is overprotective or domineering and you can avoid returning to that environment, you may want to consider getting your own apartment or staying with a friend.

Your self-confidence will be fragile and shaky at first. You need to be around healthy people who can nurture you in a way that encourages you to make your own decisions. You do not need to be around people who want to influence you with their hidden agendas. This can be very terrifying because it will remind you of the manipulation of the cult.

Setting the Environment

When a bone is broken, it is important to have it "set" properly. The bone is going to start healing whether it is set or not. If it is set correctly, it will be restored to its previous ability. Some say, once a broken bone heals, it is stronger where it was broken. In those early weeks, if the bone is improperly set or damaged again, it may not heal correctly.

So it is with you. You have been through a trauma. You need an environment that is conducive to helping you heal. It should feel and be safe. The people you are around should be emotionally healthy people. If you are around emotionally unhealthy people, the "bone" may set incorrectly. You may find yourself with other problems later on that aren't related to the cult experience, but were assimilated from those overprotective and domineering people during those critical early months of recovery.

You may not have a choice where you live, but by being aware of the effect of your environment during those early months, you can help offset any negative effects and "milk" the healthy ones.

Rest and Food

Get plenty of it! Being in a cult is very stressful; so is leaving a cult. The stress is so severe for many, if not most, ex-cultists that it is really not stress at all, but trauma. The difference between stress and trauma is the difference between falling off your bicycle and falling from a second story window. You have been traumatized and it is going to take time to heal. Under these conditions, it's very normal to have trouble sleeping or to sleep a great deal. It's normal to eat a lot of certain foods or not to be hungry. Remember, you're working through a major traumatic life event.

The stress while being in a cult has been known to stop menstrual cycles in women and beard growth in men. Mind control can have very powerful physiological and occasionally even hallucinogenic effects. Therefore, when you leave the cult and if you can at all afford it or a free or low income clinic is available, consider having a complete medical checkup. This is especially true if you were in a cult that ate a restrictive diet, or used drugs or sex to recruit or to control followers. If you have not been getting regular dental and eye exams, consider these as well. You should do this for yourself, the kids, and all other family members who left with you.

For those who were in abusive groups that shunned health care professionals, it may be scary to go for a checkup. You could use a checkup as an opportunity to challenge some of the residual anxieties and phobias. Here's how you might try it.

A Visit to the Doctor's Office

Use the buddy system. Try taking someone with you to the doctor's office, clinic, or medical center and talk about what you're feeling as you go. (This method would work if you decide to go to a psychologist's office, too.) You may want to allow some extra time so you can stop and relax, if need be. If you'd like, talk with the nurse and/or doctor before the appointment and explain that you are phobic toward doctors but would like to overcome your fear. A good health care professional will take the time to be understanding and accepting of your feelings. It may also help to have someone show you around the office or medical center and explain what will be done and why.

The result of taking the time and energy to respond to your fear, rather than react to it, is to validate your feelings and the experiences that have caused these feelings and to break down these fears so that they don't encumber you in the future.

Nutritional Needs

Some cults served healthy food, but not enough of the right foods for such a stressful lifestyle. (Stress can come from too little stimulation as well as from too much.) Some cults had followers eating garbage — another good reason for a checkup. Whatever your group ate, check that you are getting the right amounts of a well-balanced diet now.

Your body may have different nutritional needs while under the stress of recovery. If you're not sure what makes for good nutrition, check out the library or a medical center. Moderate regular exercise, such as walking, is also very helpful in regulating the body during this stressful time.

Forbidden Foods

Some ex-cultists can be completely immobilized by the presence of foods once banned by the cult. This can be very embarrassing if you're over to dinner at a friend's house or out with company. It's okay to be afraid, but you will benefit from eventually disassembling many of these fears. One way to try dismantling food phobias is to find out if you're allergic to the "forbidden foods" or if the foods really do pose a legitimate health hazard to you. If not and if you want to, consider trying to overcome the fear and any residual control of the cult by trying the "forbidden foods." The food practices of the cult may have sensitized your body to certain foods, so monitor your body's reactions if you choose to expand your food selection.

My body had a hunger for hamburgers when I first returned home. I found myself eating three big hamburgers a night, three or four times a week for about a month shortly after returning home. After a while, my hunger for the additional meat subsided. Others have told me similar stories.

You can and should hold onto the good that you acquired in the cult. This may include changes in eating habits. Some ex-cultists' eating habits improved in the cult. Some became vegetarians while in the cult and chose to remain so after leaving. Whatever your eating habits are now, make sure you and those who left with you are getting the proper nutrition. It will help you heal.

More Information, Please!

The mind has the capacity to do some amazing things (Ornstein & Thompson, 1984), such as reason, deduction, assessment, judgment, and evaluation. These abilities enable the individual to take conflicting and/or related pieces of information and process them. The cults place inhibitors in the mind during the conversion process to stop these functions from operating and to stop the internal flow of information. These inhibitors have been implanted by ideas or false reason. Without proper counseling, these inhibitors can remain in the mind and distort a person's thinking for years.

One of the toughest jobs in recovery is to reclaim or develop these mental faculties or learned skills of thinking. One way to teach yourself the art of thinking is by asking "gray" questions, questions which do not have a black or white or easily recognized answer (see Where is This on the Gray Scale?, p. 40). This process of reclaiming, rebuilding, and strengthening one's mental faculties takes discipline. It takes discipline to reclaim the mind after the cult has driven it into a deep freeze.

Doing Your Homework

Information is the food and thinking is the exercise with which you can strengthen the mind. Thinking will enable you to wade through all the issues leaving a cult can raise. When I returned from the cult, my father kept saying "do your homework, do your homework." I did, though not as extensively as he had wished, and it is this same advice that I pass on to others: do your homework. (See Appendices B and C, and the Recommended Reading and Reference Lists.)

In my years of working with ex-cultists and their families, I have seen one common problem that keeps tripping them up—they don't study mind control techniques thoroughly. They read articles and books and watch videos, but do not really study and work the materials as if their life depended on it, yet it does. Ex-cultists need a very high level of competence with the materials in order to break free of the residual mind control and cult-induced phobias. The family needs this level of competence to help the ex-cultist continue to break free once home.

Parents want to get their child out of the clutches of the cult, assuming everything can then get back to normal. Once out, the problem is solved. Right? Wrong! Remember, intervention is only the *beginning* of the recovery process. The more the ex-cultist and the family do their homework, the faster and more thorough the recovery can be.

Talk with other ex-cultists, if possible, consider a rehab facility, watch videos, go to lectures, give lectures, take a course or two, get information about mind control techniques and how they work as well as information on the cult itself. At the end of this book is a recommended reading list. I have found it is more helpful to read a few books very thoroughly then to read every book on the subject. I have read and reread at least a few chapters each year since I left the cult in 1980.

Insufficient Understanding

Even when I warn families about the problem of insufficient understanding, they still don't study enough. Why? Possibly because studying is hard work. Possibly because families may mistakenly think that understanding mind control is the ex-cultist's responsibility not theirs. They think they did their part by getting the loved one out of the cult. But this is not enough. To really be helpful, the family should understand how mind control works.

Another reason some families shy away from gaining a truly in-depth understanding of how abusive groups work is that the reality of mind control can challenge the very foundation of why you believe what you believe about everything. It can change forever the way you interact with the world around you.

When Have I Studied Enough?

One gauge I use to answer the question "how much studying is enough?" is that you have studied enough when:

1. The experience has no more hold on your ability to live the life you want to live.
2. You can explain the experience to other persons so they can understand it.
3. You can explain mind control to other persons so they understand how and why it could happen to them.

As I said, most ex-cultists and their families and their support systems in general stop doing their homework too soon. They get a little bit of knowledge and begin to stop hurting, so they stop learning and reworking the experience. Let me suggest you do yourself a really big favor and don't be one of these people. Read, talk, and write again and again until you understand how it happened and how to prevent it (See Andersen & Zimbardo, 1984).

Learn to Tell Your Story

Understanding the experience to the point you can explain it to someone else is not as simple as it may sound. First, you need to understand mind control techniques; and, secondly, you need to learn how to *effectively* communicate this information to others.

Many ex-cultists, especially in the early months, try to get anyone and everyone to comprehend the experience. This is not effective communication. Some, a bit less tactful, even try to cram comprehension down the throats of their listeners. Like a bull in a china shop, they do an "information dump" on anyone within range. If the listener doesn't understand, the ex-cultist gets frustrated and angry and/or judges the listener to be a fool. Those listeners who do manage to understand something out of this barrage are usually overwhelmed and frightened when they leave the discussion. This is not a healthy or responsible method of teaching others about cults.

I fought this "I need to make you understand" battle for a while, too. I felt guilty when I left people frightened and like a freak when they simply couldn't understand. I finally figured out what I was doing wrong. I wasn't *assessing* the listener. I wasn't really talking to that particular person. I thought I was, but I wasn't. I had to admit I wasn't, because the listener wasn't grasping what I was trying to say.

Talk "With" Not "At"

So, I challenged myself to get better at communicating, to develop better communication and presentation skills. I challenged myself to talk *with* not *at* listeners, to assess by their body language, questions, and expressions how much to tell and how much to leave for another time. I used humor and openness, and set a goal of leaving the listener with just a couple of points well-understood. This is not manipulation. It's respecting people and the different ways they learn.

It was hard at first, but I learned. As I learned and changed how I talked with others and how much I said, I found that I communicated more effectively. As I communicated more effectively, I found a great deal of understanding, empathy, and support from many people.

The most effective technique was to spend most of the conversation helping listeners recognize their own vulnerabilities and needs. Put listeners in touch with their own loneliness, sense of uselessness, or hunger for love, and it's very easy to follow up with "well, what if I offered you the answer to your problems..." Once listeners understood that it could happen to them, teaching them how mind control works was pretty straightforward. (See Carnegie, 1936.)

You will find many people who are easily frightened by your story. The truth that given the right set of circumstances they, too, could be psychologically manipulated and lose their freedom to choose does not fit with their model of how the world is supposed to work. To understand your story they have to change some of their fundamental perceptions of life. This is very hard work for anyone to do. Be patient and gentle with these people.

Letting the Steam Out

There is a point in recovery, usually early on, when you're overwhelmed with anger and energy by the experience. You may find yourself compulsively talking to anyone who appears to be listening. This is very normal and can be a very constructive part of healing. Here is where family and friends can be a great help, just by listening patiently. This need to "tell all" seems to occur for a few weeks or months until the energy runs out. Then the need to have others understand becomes more important.

Time for Pondering

It helps, when your brain has been "on hold" for so long, to take time to ponder, wonder, and reflect about things.

In cults, reflection is usually dangerous and painful. Thoughts and doubts which challenge the teachings are shameful. There is also a sense of betraying the leader. This shame inhibits critical thinking. No thinking means no mental exercise. No mental exercise means atrophy. To rebuild the mind, the ex-cultist needs to reflect upon information, wonder about how pieces fit together, and ponder ideas.

The challenge to thinking, however, is that as you ponder you may find yourself coming up with new and different conclusions about many things. It takes courage to face these reflections honestly and not to run away from them or hide behind a myth. There are many long-established myths deeply rooted in our culture which can cause confusion and pose scary contradictions for the ex-cultist. (See Letting Go of Myths, p. 59.)

As time went by, I found myself scrutinizing *everything* I believed in, such as religion (what is God now), the purpose of government (why isn't it more effective and why doesn't it get rid of the cults), the purpose of language, the responsibility of friends, trust (how could I ever trust anyone again), and more. Wading through all this reevaluation caused despair. The only way out of this despair was to keep thinking and to keep getting in touch with my feelings, reworking it all, letting go of myths until life began to make a little more sense.

Society at a Crossroads

When you leave the cult, you are not entering a healthy society. There are pockets of healthy people and families, but in my opinion American society has a tendency to deny, rationalize, and seek quick fixes to problems.

As you struggle to put your life back together, to find meaning and purpose, to understand the cult experience, to develop new skills, you will be struggling through this slow and painful process in a society addicted to quick fixes and afraid of pain. You do not have an easy task ahead of you. We can be thankful that more and more people in America are coming to terms with the necessity to put time and effort into solving problems.

Pre-Cult Developmental Issues

Remember, too, that any unresolved developmental issues from before the cult will resurface and will need to be worked through. If available, a well-trained therapist can be helpful. For those who were in therapeutic or encounter cults, any type of counseling may simply be too loaded for a while. At some point, though, it might be helpful to learn to trust a therapeutic relationship again, although you may want to avoid therapsts who support New Age encounter cults.

Also available and often at little or no cost are support groups for many different types of problems, including such painful and difficult issues as incest, alcoholism and the adult children of alcoholics, rape, and more. (See Black, 1982; Vaughan, 1982; Whitfield, 1987; Woititz, 1983.)

Financial Stability

Writing a résumé, finding a job, earning money, managing a checking account, paying bills, and deciphering a bank statement may all be very new experiences for some ex-cultists. It can be overwhelming to have to acquire so many self-management skills while trying to heal, especially during the first year of recovery. Family, friends, and others can be very helpful and supportive by teaching you these necessary skills, encouraging you to become self-sufficient little by little (see Basic Skills, p. 66). If you can afford them, there are also résumé and job counseling services available.

A word of caution, the primary goal of recovery is to work through and integrate the cult experience. Be careful not to get so caught up in school or a job that you don't have the time or energy to learn about mind control and to get in touch with your feelings regarding the experience. Otherwise, these issues may surface at the wrong times, for example when you are interacting with your boss.

Work Environments

You have left an environment where you were often told what to do and how to think. Some companies are run this way and that similarity may feel very threatening to you. It could set off "floating" episodes (see Floating, p. 36) or cause you to become disoriented and anxious. If you have to work and if such a company is the only employer for your job skill, you may have little choice for now but to work for them. This, too, can cause a feeling of being helpless and manipulated.

It might help reduce this stress, if you decide to work in this environment only for a certain period of time, say, until you are stronger. In the meantime, discuss the events at work and your reactions with someone you trust. This will help reduce the stress, and provide support and a reality check for your reactions. As you work through the issues of recovery, you can build a job plan and look for a different work environment later.

Routine and Boring

When I was still in the early stages of recovery and needed a job, it was suggested to me to find a dull, routine job where I wouldn't have to think too much, but one that would give my life some structure. This was a very helpful suggestion, because when the depression and grieving set in, I was very overwhelmed trying to work through my feelings. If I had had a demanding job at the same time, it would have been too much stress for me. Later, as I healed and began to acquire good thinking skills, I was able to plan my career and my personal goals to provide more challenge and excitement.

The retired elderly who have left abusive groups may find volunteer work a helpful way to make friends. It will also provide structure.

Interviews and Résumés

What do you say when the interviewer asks: "How do you account for this gap in employment?" Depending on your assessment of the interviewer, you can either talk around the cult experience or talk to it. I've given several different answers to this question, such as:

- I was in a cult. Usually not a very good response.
- I was off trying to save the world, but it didn't work (laugh, laugh). If delivered well this can be effective.
- I was implementing training programs for a religious group I worked for. This was often the best choice.

An employer is usually looking for an honest, reliable, stable, and hardworking employee, who can get along with the rest of the department. Everyone gets kicked down in life sooner or later and a good employer knows and accepts this. An employer is often more concerned with how well you handled the problem and how you are doing now.

How do you rewrite your résumé? Here's what I've done:

TRAINER, Therapy, Inc., Goingnowhere Town, State
Implemented religious training programs of varying length
and complexity to audiences throughout the U.S., involving
multimedia formats designed to teach religious issues and
leadership development. Graduated from a leadership
development program and provided counseling to devotees.

Exercise–Job Interview Skills

Practice the interview process with a family member or friend. Try role playing and try both roles. See if you can get a feel for what the interviewer might want in a candidate by learning about the company, their product(s), and their competition. Write down some questions you think you might be asked and work out answers to those questions. Present yourself favorably. You should feel good about yourself, because you are handling a tough recovery problem well.

Talking about the Cult at Work

It can be confusing trying to figure out whom you should or can talk to about the cult experience. In the cult you had to confess all and not keep anything to yourself. If you did hold something back, you were shamed and considered deceitful and disloyal. This technique was used to reinforce your dependence on the group. Now, you do not have to tell everyone everything. You do not have to tell people about your cult experience, and you don't have to hide it either. However, you do need to learn to assess *when and with whom* it is appropriate to talk about your experience. This is true at work as well as elsewhere.

It is often not appropriate to talk about your experiences at work, at least until you get *very good* at how to do it without overwhelming and frightening people. For the first several months, you may want to concentrate on just two things: doing the task and getting along with others. As you get to know people and you feel comfortable with them, you can try building a friendship and trusting them: first with little bits of your story, and, if they prove themselves supportive and understanding, you can later trust them with more.

Early in recovery you will want to tell everyone about what happened to you. This is normal. However, try to "let the steam out" with people outside of work until you are comfortable with how to tell your story.

Working with a Cultist

This slow approach to talking about your cult experience at work is also helpful considering that some of the people you work with may be in a cult. You don't need to save them. You need to take care of yourself first.

If you decide you want to confront someone about his or her cult involvement, assess whether others in the office are also in this cult, and, if so, what any confrontation on your part will do to your job security. If you decide you want to continue, invite the person off the work site and mention that you have heard that their group may have some questionable practices. If the person is interested in knowing more (be careful that this is not merely a recruiting tactic), offer to give or to get information.

If you are going to confront cultists, realize that you should also be willing to take some responsibility for helping them with recovery. You cannot open the door and then leave them stranded. It is my opinion that you should first take care of your own recovery and then later reach out to others. (See Getting Healthy to Help Others, p. 40.)

Summary

It is extremely painful to realize that those who have professed to love and care for you have, in truth, exploited and used you for their own gain. There is, however, a great sense of relief in getting away from the excessive demands, intimidation, and manipulation of the group and its leader(s). Leaving is filled with difficult emotions. The experience has been a trauma to the self. Once you are out, it is necessary to integrate the experience and thereby heal the self.

Chapter 2:
Phase Two–Understanding and Feeling

*All the flowers of all the tomorrows are in the seeds
of today.*
—Unknown

Phase One is usually a dawning process of several days or months, possibly years. Phase Two, however, is full of ups and downs. It can span months or years depending on many of the factors noted in the Introduction. Because I was also dealing with a rape and with codependency issues related to my family background, Phase Two for me has taken about eight years. It is my hope that sharing my struggles and ideas with you will help to shorten your recovery. (See Branden, 1971; Bridges, 1980; Hassan, 1988; Langone, 1993; Singer, 1979; Stoner and Kisser, 1992; Whitfield, 1987.)

It is my belief that it doesn't have to take that long. With more counselors trained about cults, more recovered ex-cultists articulating their experiences, and more information available on recovery, this phase may take much less time. If you are a victim of rape or incest, are obsessive/compulsive, codependent and/or a substance abuser or otherwise troubled, you will need to address and integrate these issues as well for a full recovery. (See Vaughan, 1982; Whitfield, 1987; Woititz, 1983.)

Reconnecting with Family and Friends

What do you do when you've been on another planet for up to 20 years or more and you've just returned home? You feel like Rip Van Winkle. Everyone you know, if they are even still around, is older and at a different place in life. Family and friends are often further along in their education and/or career. They may be married, divorced, own a home, or run a business. Not only may you feel like a freak for having been in a cult, but you may feel inadequate when looking at the accomplishments of an old chum.

Looking Foolish

What if you tried to recruit the friend? You may feel embarrassed and apologetic. What if you threatened him with eternal damnation for not having embraced "the truth"? Well, you eat crow. You learn how to apologize, explain, ask for help, and laugh at yourself. I've been so embarrassed by the cult experience and the phobias it left in me that I feel permanently humbled. I'm not afraid to look foolish anymore, at least about the cult experience.

I tried to recruit Jean, my long-time best friend. The only reason she didn't follow me in was that she didn't have the money for the introductory class. Thank goodness. She had missed having me around all those years I was off "saving the world," missed having her old friend around to talk things out with. I felt guilty, sad, and angry at the time we'd lost. I explained that I had been tricked, and she understood. Sometimes, she'd ask me about the cult experience or why I didn't leave, and we'd talk. It was great to have her around when I came home even though I didn't feel as if I knew her very well, having been gone for so many years. No other friends were left.

Revisiting to Fill the Void

I'd missed other things, too. I'd missed my brothers' football games, and proms, ski trips with family and friends, and birthdays. The cult had stolen these things from me and there was a hole inside of me. For awhile, it seemed as if nothing could fill that hole. It was as if there was this huge gap between who I was the day I was recruited and who I was the day I left. Either alone or with friends, it did help to revisit people and places I had known before my cult experience. Revisiting helped to close that gap. It helped me to bridge backward so the present was more stable and connected, more integrated.

Missed Events

Some ex-cultists, because of the constraints of the cult, missed critical life events with families and friends, such as births, deaths, marriages, religious observances, and graduations. Remember, it was the psychological controls and demands of the cult that kept you from participating in these events. Thus, it may help you to discuss this loss with the family and to hear that the family has forgiven you. Forgive yourself, too, and grieve the loss of not having been a part of these events. You handled your responsibilities as best you could under mind control. Blame the cult, not yourself.

The Good, the Bad, and the Ugly

For some ex-cultists who go home after exiting the cult, it's good to be back among loved ones. For others, the cult with all its lies offered them more than the family has. Returning home can be a mixed experience. Some families can understand mind control and accept and forgive what happened. Others continue to judge and try to control the loved one. Some families try to bury the experience, refusing to discuss what happened. These behaviors can be extremely destructive to a healthy recovery.

You need to evaluate your family's ability to understand what happened to you. If they cannot understand and be supportive, you need to grieve this loss of love and let go of expecting them to change. They may never be able to understand and accept what happened to you. It may simply be too threatening to them.

It can also be terrifying to let go of expectations of your family when you have already let go of the cult, but there are other support systems available to you. You need to take some time to identify them and evaluate whether they are good support systems for you. Support groups are listed in the telephone directory or are available by calling a local medical center, hospital, or your doctor. FOCUS specifically addresses the needs of ex-cultists.

As painful as it is to come to terms with a family's lack of acceptance and support, when you are ready, grieve and let go. Don't waste what energy you do have for recovery trying to make the deaf hear.

Exercise–Family Assessment

List those in your family and extended family who are available for support. What is it about each person that can be helpful to you? What are their strengths (example: empathetic, fun to be with, good thinker)? What weaknesses does each have that might make it difficult for you to interact with them (example: impatient, judgmental)?

Making New Friends

If you were not very good at making friends before you were recruited into the cult, you may have trouble still. Others did so much recruiting and teaching that they are now very comfortable talking to strangers. The hardest part of making new friends for most ex-cultists is threefold:

1. Trusting anyone ever again
2. Explaining the cult experience
3. Letting it take time

Ex-cultists who have spent most of their life within a cult will need to learn the basic social skills of making friends and interacting with people. How to interact with people when not recruiting them? How to accept a request for a date or how to ask someone out on a date? How to know what you need and to negotiate for what is appropriate for you within relationships?

One of the problems with making friends is that in most cults everyone had been an instant friend, an instant brother and sister, an instant family. (The instant, perfect family—marketing the cult as a fast fix in a fast-food society.) But relationships are not formed instantly in the real world and for very good reasons. Not everyone is trustworthy to the same degree. Not everyone needs friendship in the same way. Not everyone sees their responsibility in a friendship the same way. In the real world, people can be very different. The challenge in making new friends is to assess the differences, and this takes time.

Build Trust Slowly

It can be very hard to trust people after you have been so betrayed by the cult. It's helpful and important to realize, though, that in a real friendship you build trust with someone. This is a very different idea from the instant-fix idea of the cults. Building something takes time. Building trust means that you trust a little bit at a time and then check that your trust is being honored and returned by the other person. Then you trust a little more, check; trust a little more, check, etc.

If you're lonely and in pain from the experience, which often happens, the temptation can be to trust wholly and all at once. This can be like Russian roulette. If the person is emotionally mature and trustworthy, you're pretty safe trusting them. If they have some psychological problems and are not trustworthy, then you will be hurt again and discouraged. Here is where you need to learn to *evaluate the person's trustworthiness.*

Behavior and Words

What do you look for in order to evaluate someone's trustworthiness? Check to see if the behavior matches the words. This is the first check. For example, if you are meeting someone is he or she on time? If not, is he or she honest about the reason for being late? Does he admit it is a bad habit or does he rationalize? Often someone who rationalizes is not honest with himself and, therefore, cannot be honest with you.

What happens when people are late because they got stuck in traffic. Is this rationalization? If your cult taught, as mine did, that getting stuck in traffic is your fault because you weren't listening to God (or whatever), then you might find yourself reacting to your friend's reason for being late as if you were still in the cult. You might discredit the person and tell yourself he is not very trustworthy (he is too "weak"), when really what's needed is to untangle more of the cult's teachings.

This is a pretty good example of how subtle recovery can get. Examining your thinking and conclusions is what I mean by mental discipline.

Sometimes it's like untangling a ball of string the cat's been playing with – time-consuming, frustrating, and exasperating.

Making new friends provides many opportunities not only for the love and support of others, but also for the interactions that can help to highlight your own faulty reasoning and residual ideological cobwebs.

Where are They?

Where are these new friends? I found many in a community chorus I got involved with after returning home. I'd always loved singing and needed to reconnect with that part of myself. As I went to rehearsal every week, spoke with people at break, and performed in concerts in the area, I began to feel part of the local community. I would run into someone at the grocery store and say "hi." Slowly, I didn't feel quite so isolated and lonely. (See Carnegie, 1936.)

As I got to know a few people, and would hear their life stories, I realized that others have had great pain, too. Maybe a miscarriage, infidelity, lost job, death of a child, assault, theft, and other misfortunes helped me to put my experience in perspective. I tried never to minimize my experience, but was able to learn from others how to cope with crisis, integrate it, learn from it, and then go on with life.

Try Something New

Try a new hobby or sport. Take a course at the local community college. Try dancing or music or help out at a community theatre production. If you're not comfortable going alone, invite a family member or friend. After so many years of not having you around, they may be glad for the opportunity to be with you again. Is there a local art show, little league, or town fair? Maybe offer to help.

Exercise–Reconnecting

List the interests, activities, and sports that you were involved with before the group experience (example: thespian, musician, hockey)? What role did you play in these activities (example: stage manager, flutist, goalie)? Which activities did you enjoy the most? What was it about the activity that you liked? What outlets for your interests are available in your community? What new interests might you enjoy pursuing?

Small Talk

If you notice someone you'd like to meet, engage in small talk. You may feel awkward at first, as if you're setting them up to be recruited. I felt this way for a while, too. I also felt uncomfortable with small talk because it seemed trivial.

I have come to appreciate, though, that small talk is a key part of *evaluating listeners,* as well as helping them to assess you. When you make small talk, there are actually several things going on:

- You are identifying common interests. Instead of jumping into an instant friendship, you can evaluate whether or not you have enough in common with this person to make the effort worthwhile to you.

- You are identifying personality styles. In the real world people are different. They approach problems differently and interact with others differently. You may not want to become friends with someone who approaches life too differently from you. On the other hand, you may be tired of the same types of people and want a friend who offers a different perspective and approach to life. For example, you may be shy and feel bullied around someone too aggressive. You may be very analytical and find yourself annoyed with someone who would rather be friendly than think about a problem. You may be people-oriented and would feel bored and intimidated with someone who is task-oriented.

- You are assessing their credibility. What are their life and work experiences? How do they know about the subject you're both discussing? Can they look you in the eye while you are talking? Are they listening to you when you speak or do they want to do all the talking? Do they interrupt frequently? How do they respond to what you're saying? Are they supportive, critical, judgmental, or validating?

Small talk enables you to evaluate people before you confide in them too deeply and trust them only to be later disappointed. It may be called "small talk," but it can be an important part of evaluating people's credibility.

Yes, I'd Like to Get to Know You

If you decide you want to get to know someone better, you could ask him or her out for coffee. Remember, let it take time. You don't have to recruit them into the local chorus group if you don't want to, and you don't have to talk about the cult experience if you don't want to. Most people love to talk about themselves. If you ask them a couple of questions that cannot be answered with a simple yes or no, they may well talk your ear off. Making and developing friendships can provide healthy support systems and be an interesting way of exploring what life has to offer by seeing what works for others.

I should warn you that some people prey on others who have been hurt. They appear friendly and then use you. You know this because you were in a cult, but these types of people are still around you. When you're first out and fragile, be wary, especially of situations that may have sexual overtones. I'm sad to say that some ex-cultists have even trusted other ex-cultists only to find later they have been used.

Be a wise consumer. Ask other people to help you evaluate someone. This is a good reality check method to use throughout your life.

Answering Questions

Let me go back to something I just said—you don't have to talk about the cult experience if you don't want to. I didn't say this to suggest you don't talk about it. But often ex-cultists feel as if they have to do whatever they are asked to do, or feel they have to answer any question they are asked. In my cult we used to say, "don't ask how high, just jump."

Cultists are manipulated into unquestioned obedience. If someone asks a question, you answer it. If you don't want to, there is something wrong with you. Either you don't trust the doctrine or you are hiding something evil. Some ex-cultists continue to face the same dilemma: I've got to tell all or there's something wrong with me, yet I don't want to tell all.

Ex-cultists often avoid situations that could help them develop and relearn assessment skills because on some level they still believe they have to obey any request of them, even a question. You don't have to do what anyone wants you to do anymore without thinking it through, assessing its value to you, and evaluating how to handle the situation.

Assessing the Question

You can start learning this process of assessment with any question someone asks of you. Ask yourself:

- Do I want to talk about this with this person at this time? If not, would I be comfortable answering it at a later date or not at all?
- If I decide to answer the question, is this person trustworthy and intelligent enough to use the information in a responsible manner?

If you're having trouble sorting out how you feel and there is time, try talking it over with someone you trust. Talking it over will also help you stay focused on the question, if you're having trouble concentrating.

When you've sorted your thoughts and feelings out, then let the person know what's going on. "I'm not really comfortable answering that question right now. Maybe we could talk about it later."

It's important to realize that now you can determine your behavior. Yet, it's also important to help others understand where you're coming from in order to avoid misunderstandings. It may take time to unlearn unquestioned obedience.

Spouse Involved

The cult tried to recruit you and your spouse. After awhile, you walked away but your spouse is still involved. The one you love and pledged your life to has changed almost beyond recognition, certainly beyond reason. You have children to consider and to protect. What to do?

If you can, consider setting up an intervention. If you are one of the lucky ones, he or she may be talked out. Involve your family, friends, and the children. Build a knowledgeable supportive environment for your spouse to come home to. For many others, however, the involvement of a spouse causes divorce and a custody battle over the children. If this is your situation, here are some ideas. Be sure to take care of yourself. Your well-being is critical. (For information on the legal implications of child custody when a cult is involved see Kandell, 1987/88 and Greene, 1989 noted in the Additional Readings list.)

Avoid a Battleground!

If during the divorce settlement, she got the children *avoid a battleground!* Get help from family, friends and a therapist, if needed, on this because it is really very important to avoid battling. You'll lose and so will the children. Don't confront her on cult issues. To best negoitiate, talk in terms of what she needs to continue her cult activities. For example, if the children are living with her, instead of battling to have the children, help her realize that to have more time to meditate, you will agree to spend additional time with the children and this will free up her schedule. (See Carnegie, 1936.)

Kids Gotta Love

Children will love their parent whether she is in a cult or not. Accept that the children need to be able to love their parent and have a relationship with her. Don't battle with the children or play their love for her against their love for you.

Except for cases of child abuse or neglect, very young children often survive living with a cult parent reasonably well. You can help give the child the love and affection the cult parent will be too busy to give. You can discuss mom's behavior with the child and help him or her understand what is real.

As children get older, they will probably be embarrassed by mom meditating in the family room and not invite friends over during this time or usher their friends in the side door. Like children of an alcoholic parent, they may get too good at pushing their embarrassment, confusion, sadness, loneliness, and anger into the background. You can help them understand and express their feelings. You will probably need to be the one to bring the subject up.

Talk about mom's behavior and explain that her behavior is not because of the children but because of her involvement in the cult. For example, when mom doesn't have any money for a Saturday matinee, explain that it is because mom gave it to the cult. You can help them fulfill their need to love her and, yet, help them understand that they do not have to agree with what she is doing.

Sometimes, the situation is not amenable to the suggestions I have made. In these cases, consult a therapist who understands cults.

You're OK; They're OK

The children will often do as well as you do. If you are in turmoil, anger, and worry, it will make it harder on the children and it will take its toll on you. Use your energy constructively and have faith in your children. Take care of yourself! Check out your library for books on children and divorce. Talk out your feelings with others. There will be hurts and bruises within for your children, but as long as you can talk with them, you can help them through these difficult times.

Flashbacks

A flashback is an interruption of the present with an incident from the past. It is not uncommon to remember sights, sounds, smells, faces, and feelings from such a powerful and pervasive experience as a cult involvement. Often the emotions that accompany the flashback or that are stirred up by the flashback are overwhelming. For example, many of us were told by a group leader that we would die if we left the group. A flashback of seeing the leader's face could produce feelings of anxiety and fear, sometimes to the point of immobilization. Excessive or uncontrollable flashbacks are the signal that professional help is needed to work out residual underlying fears, phobias, or anxieties.

Flashbacks affected me on only a few occasions, but they were even stirred up again while writing this handbook many years later. Sounds and faces were the most reccurring form for me. I'd be walking down the street and a dozen or so of the faces I walked past would remind me of those I had left behind. Sounds on the radio, not whole songs but just short phrases of sound, would remind me of the cult's music and musicians. Flashbacks occurred most frequently when I was under emotional stress.

The only way I've found to work through these episodes is to talk about them with someone, preferably another ex-cultist. If I tried to avoid the reality of these gnats and keep them to myself, I'd get disoriented and frightened. They could be so persistent. But talking seemed to "let the air out" of them. While talking, I'd try to pinpoint the underlying feelings I had and work them through. Also, when under stress, I try to get lots of sleep, eat well, and not keep feelings bottled up.

Floating

When you're recruited into a cult, a cult personality or identity is superimposed onto your own personality. The cult reinforces and strengthens this cult identity through chanting and meditation, the restriction of language, and through information control—both from external sources and internally by cutting off certain mental functions, such as reflection and reason. (See Hoffer, 1966; Lifton, 1969.)

As the years go by, the cult personality remains dominant, successfully reinforced by the cult. The old you is there but quietly buried (for some not so quietly) waiting to be freed, like a bird in a cage. Once a person becomes aware of the psychological controls the cult has used and of the discrediting information about the cult and its leaders, the follower begins to reuse the mind and much of the old personality begins to emerge from hibernation.

That old personality is shaky at first for some, and often individuals find themselves "floating" between the old cult identity and the new self. In this between state, questions arise which can be confusing and frightening. "Should I stay out or should I go back?" "Is being out of the cult really the right thing to do?" This indecision seems so odd, for just a few hours ago the ex-cultist was quite firm about the resolution to leave such a deceitful and manipulative group. How to handle the situation?

Monitoring Stress

The stress of the recovery process can bring on floating incidents. Recovery is hard work. It can seem lonely and scary at times as well as exciting. Pre-existing psychological problems are still awaiting resolution. It's normal to feel overwhelmed. In the midst of all this work and struggle, you may find yourself thinking "wouldn't it be easier to go back?"

When this happened to me, I would say to myself "yes, it would be easier to go back, but I wasn't really happy there. In fact, I was emotionally and psychologically abused there. I want to learn how to handle my life now. I don't want to go back into the fog." Reciting these words to myself would help. I also made sure to get lots of rest and to talk with someone about what I was feeling.

Try to identify when the floating incidents occur. What is happening that may be causing these episodes? Floating may most often occur when you're facing a lot of emotional stress. It's important to learn to recognize the signs of stress in your body, mind, and emotions. You can then monitor how much stress to try and handle. Hunger and fatigue are good examples of your body sending signals. (See Appendix A.)

Exercise–Learning to Recognize Signals

Write down the answers to the following questions: What does your physical body need to survive (example: air, water)? What signals does your body send when it does not get enough of each one? What signals does your body send when it does get enough of each one?

What does your mind need to be healthy (example: stimulation, discipline, rest)? What signals does your mind send when it does not get enough of each one? What signals does your mind send when it does get enough of each one?

What does your heart (soul) need to be healthy (example: security, love, forgiveness)? What signals does your heart (soul) send when it does not get enough of each one? What signals does your heart (soul) send when it does get enough of each one?

Emotions as Feedback Systems

As your emotions thaw and you learn to become more aware of them and what they're telling you, you can use your emotions to identify stress-inducing situations. You can then respond to that feedback in ways that will reduce stress and enrich your life. Sadness, jealousy, laughter, bemusement are all telling you things about different parts of yourself. As you learn to listen and then reflect upon what your feelings are trying to tell you about your needs, you can then integrate that information into a more whole you. As you learn what you need, you can take action to make sure you are getting enough of what it takes to meet those needs.

Look but Don't Touch

I have also had to accept that there are songs, scriptures, places, and situations that I should avoid when I'm under stress, tired, or blue.

These situations have too much potential to disorient me. By learning to monitor and moderate stress, I have usually been able to identify and avoid stress levels that bring on floating and flashback incidents.

I would also talk about what I was feeling with family and friends. Talking seemed to help defuse a floating incident and release anxiety. Remember the buddy system? Let your friends help you and don't be afraid or too embarrassed to ask for help!

Uncontrolled Floating

This is a very serious situation and does happen to some people, especially those from cults which use extensive meditation. When this happens to you, like emergency first aid, grab someone and start talking about what's going on inside your head. Talk, don't isolate yourself.

Get professional help immediately, if available, or as soon as possible. Counseling can be done over the phone or in person. An exit counselor or ex-cultist may best be able to help you sort through the problem. You are not alone. You are not crazy. You have been traumatized.

Extensive Meditation and Attention Deficiencies

Some ex-cultists from groups that used intense and prolonged chanting and meditation have a very hard time stopping this practice. It is critical to your recovery to stop chanting. To heal, you need to actively engage your mind. Chanting tunes out the mind, but you need to learn to concentrate on thinking. You can start relearning to concentrate by focusing your attention on what you are thinking about or by focusing on what someone else is saying. This is called *active listening*. You know you are listening and thinking when you have questions to ask about what's being said.

The following exercise you can try with a friend to help strengthen your attention and thinking.

Exercise–Active Listening

Try the following: Have your friend start talking about something of interest to you both, such as dating, sex, jobs, or ice cream. Have your friend make a few comments or ask a question. Stop. Ask "how does this relate to me?" Write your answer down. Have your friend continue and repeat these steps.

After about 5-15 minutes, discuss the answers with your friend. Talk about how well this exercise worked for you. If it didn't work very well for you, discuss how to modify the steps.

Do this exercise as often as you're comfortable with it. Probably once a day is good or more, if you like. You may feel pretty rusty at first, but stick with it. Unlike meditation which reduces mental activity, you are actively engaged in listening, assessing, reflecting, evaluating, critiquing, writing, articulating, and reasoning.

Home from the War

For some ex-cultists, there is from time to time a haunting feeling of having left behind others in the clutches of the cult. This is particularly true for those who recruited others. It's very normal to feel guilty about being free while so many others are in abusive groups and are being recruited daily. As you heal and learn about how the abusive psychological controls were used on you, the more anxious you can become for those left behind.

An Analogy

After I'd been out for several months, I had a lot of trouble sleeping. One night I went downstairs and huddled myself in a blanket in front of the TV. My Dad came downstairs after awhile and sat next to me. He could tell I was hurting. As we talked about the people I'd left behind, he made an analogy. He said it was as if I had been to war and then got to come home. But I had left my buddies in the trenches knowing the dangers they were facing. I wanted to feel great about being free, but it hurt to know others were still on the battlefield.

Helping Others Out

Leaving others behind is a hard issue to reconcile yourself to in such a way that you do not merely cut off your feelings. Some ex-cultists spend some period of time reaching back into the cult to try and get others out. This is normal and if handled wisely can be a very healing process. Others cannot risk it because of the possibility of harassment and brutal retaliation by the cult. Some ex-cultists cannot let go of this phase of recovery. They get stuck in having to help others get out and it consumes them. It is okay not to rescue everyone left behind. You have to give yourself permission to let go.

Instant Friends, Instant Enemies

When I got out of the cult, I tried to help those I knew who were still involved. So, I wrote a letter—a short, simple letter—which suggested that it was okay to ask questions, that God wanted us to ask questions, and that the cult was not what it appeared to be. I sent this letter to everyone in the cult whose address I could find. A couple of people wrote back and asked me what had happened. A long-time friend wrote "send me no more of these letters filled with the hateful bitterness of Satan." This hurt a great deal.

I had to face the painful fact that since I was no longer one of them, I was an untrustworthy outsider. As instantly as those friendships had been made, they were broken. Flashbacks of their faces painfully reminded me of this sad truth. As I felt the pain of their rejection, I also realized the suffering I had caused to others, when while still involved I had rejected those who had left the cult before me.

Getting Healthy to Help Others

The approach I have taken, which enables me to get through each day knowing of the destruction the cults are wreaking on those left behind, has been to trust that someday others will be freed as I have been. I know this isn't true for everyone. Many lives are ruined and others die. I have had to realize my limitations and acknowledge that I cannot help everyone. I cannot save the world anymore. I decided to put the energy of that grief and guilt into healing myself. Since I can't help everyone get out, then I will be a healthy ex-cultist and help those who have left. So, I work to be as healthy as I can to help the few that I can.

Names and faces have filtered through my thoughts over the years and I have prayed for life to watch over them. When people have asked me for help, I have tried to be there for them, balancing my needs with theirs. It isn't easy, and I can't always give. In the sorrow and guilt of leaving others on the battlefield, I realized why there is this idea of heaven, a perfect place where no one hurts and all the injustices suffered on earth are recompensed. It's a nice idea.

The cults tell you that you can have anything in life and that you can always win. This is a lie in or out of the cult and nowhere is this lie more painful to realize than in recognizing you cannot help everyone out of the cult. Life is imperfect and you have limitations. This is another loss—the myth of always being in control, of having total power. When you are ready, you need to grieve the loss of not being able to help everyone and then move on.

Where is This on the Gray Scale?

Cults are totalistic societies where how you think is reshaped into merely accepting the group's teachings. There is no "gray" in these teachings. They are black or white and accepting them is either all or nothing. All of life is as the cult has defined it. There is no middle ground. There are no shades of gray. There is a false security in this type of logic, a false comfort of thinking you're right and other people are wrong.

To help to dismantle this all-or-nothing thinking, I began to ask myself when confronted with a question or problem, *"where is this on the gray scale?"* This question became a favorite one of mine and was very helpful as I struggled to undo seven years in a black-and-white world and 17 years in an overbearing family. I found that life is full of shades of gray. To reinforce the point to myself, I wandered into a redecorating store one day and looked at the number of paint samples from white to gray to black. There were dozens of shades of color. I saw so clearly that, indeed, there is more to life than black or white.

Practice a Sliding Scale

You can practice finding the gray in any question. For example, "should I have one piece of toast or two?" Why not one and a half? "Should I go to the concert or stay at home?" Why not go to the concert and leave early if you decide you want to? "Should I be happy or sad?" Why not somewhere in between? In between can seem strange after so many years in a black-and-white world, but you can learn to tolerate and feel safe with gray. Try saying "I can be safe even if I don't have all the answers or know someone who does."

Getting Comfortable with Ambiguity

Ambiguity was not tolerated in the cults. You're either one of "us" or one of "them." You are either in the cult mind set or you are out of alignment. There was no such thing as a little bit this way or that. No gray was allowed. Many of us were fried by this intensity. Thoughts and feelings having no room for expression were sent into a deep freeze. Many people, who have never been in cults, are similarly locked up.

But life is *full* of ambiguity. Life is *full* of color and each color has a wide range of shades. Getting used to ambiguity takes time. As you become comfortable with gray, a much more colorful world will open up to you—more colorful and more complex.

In time you can learn to handle complex and ambiguous questions. It can be scary at first to live where the answers are not clear and quick. Part of getting comfortable with gray answers involves learning decision-making skills and then gaining experience in using these skills. (See Decision-Making.)

Dating

Dating was a very controlled and often prescribed experience in my group. Fellow groupies were often referred to as "brother" and "sister."

Such relationships made it easier to keep sexual hormones in check. In many cults, mates were assigned by the leaders or mates came only from a select subgroup within the cult.

For many, it was a relief once in the cult not to have to deal with getting a date. The instant brother/sister relationships or assigned partners took away all the anxiety that many of us face when finding a companion. In addition, physical intimacy was often controlled and often not allowed. Now, how does a person get a date and how does one behave on a date?

Behaviors

The same thoughtful, respectful, and honest behaviors that contribute to making and maintaining friendships are the cornerstone of dating, too. Let your intentions be known. Be honest. There are times when all a person wants is quick safe sex. If that's what you want, admit it to yourself and to your date. Remember, though, that you and your date may not be as able to discuss intentions as is needed. So, take it slow, practice, and be caring and alert.

There are many ways to identify someone with whom you'd like to spend more time. Generally, when you're doing what you like to do and having a good time, you'll attract and meet people. Try new activities, join a local bird watchers or hiking club, ask your friends for contacts. There are dating services, personal ads in newspapers and magazines, electronic computer dating conferences and, my favorite, the Classical Music Lovers Exchange.

Be wise and be careful. Don't get into a car with someone you don't know well. Don't meet someone in a secluded place, if you don't know him well. Have your friends "check him out." Take your time.

Relationships

To establish a friendship, take time to get to know the person, his or her interests and ideas. It helps, and makes it easier, if you have taken the time to know yourself first. If you are uncomfortable, why not share that information with your date as you would a friend? When you are comfortable, so will your date be and you'll both have a better time together. It's going to take practice. You're going to feel awkward at times. Don't worry about making mistakes.

Talk honestly and listen carefully to what your date says and doesn't say. Ask questions. Practice safe sex when and if that's on the menu.

Sex

Each ex-cultist was exposed to different experiences and information about sex while in the cult. Some were very isolated from any information about sex and basic health issues. My comments here are for those who were isolated from basic information.

Sex is a pretty loaded issue these days even if you haven't been in a cult. Sex can be particularly loaded for ex-cultists, because some abusive groups use sex to recruit members or to keep them in. Many cult leaders have sex with opposite and same-sex members even when they have preached abstinence to their followers. Many ex-cultists did not engage in sex while devotees, while others were coerced into sex with another follower, a group of followers, and/or the leader. Some were married within the cult and were given only certain dates and times when they could engage in sex.

A Few Pointers

It is very common for ex-cultists either to shy away from and fear sex, especially if it was taboo in the cult, or be promiscuous. However you choose to behave now, I offer a few pointers:

1. First, you are making memories and affecting the life of another person in a unique way. Make memories you will want to keep by being sensitive, respectful, and responsible about sharing sex. The golden rule is timeless.

2. Second, practice safe sex. Casual sex today is potentially deadly. That doesn't mean you can't share sex, but you must practice safe sex or risk killing yourself and anyone else with whom you are physically intimate.

3. Third, avoid excessive drinking with sex. Don't let alcohol impair your judgment about practicing safe sex! You don't want an unplanned pregnancy or a sexually transmitted disease to impair your recovery.

Easy Does It

If you are shy about sex or unsure about whether you want to engage in sex, that's fine, too. Take your time. It is a very special and sometimes a very vulnerable experience to open yourself up physically to another person. Take the time you need to feel comfortable and safe. Talk over your feelings with your partner, trusted friend or family member, or counselor.

If you were sexually abused before or during the cult or abused others, seek medical and/or therapeutic help. Many people also experience sexual dysfunction at some time in their life, whether in a cult or not. Take time to work out the underlying physical and/or psychological problems.

Above all, be patient and gentle with yourself. Don't let the media hype about sex and the cultural emphasis on performance push you into sex before it's what you want or in a manner that is not what you want.

Sexually Transmitted Diseases (STDs)

Some abusive groups had their followers use sex as a way to recruit new members. Some abusive groups practiced group sex. Some followers were used for sex by their leaders. If you were in a cult that practiced unsafe sex (sex without condoms or sex with multiple partners), you owe it to yourself to be checked out by a physician. There are many diseases that are transmitted sexually both orally and genitally. Not all these diseases have easily identifiable symptoms and some are very health threatening and contagious.

A visit to your doctor or the library will give you lots of good information on what these diseases are, how they are transmitted, how to detect them, and how to prevent the spread of STDs. If you are uncomfortable going to the doctor's office by yourself, take a friend with you, even into the examining room if that's what makes you feel safe.

Take care of your own body and check out your partner. Talk with your partner. Ask for his or her patience and feedback. When the checking part is over, enjoy, and learn from one another. Sex gets better with practice and good communication.

It's Okay to Ask Tough Questions

As a woman, I found that this whole issue of premeditated sex seemed unthinkable. Sex was just supposed to happen and I certainly had no right to ask, much less insist, that my boyfriend or date use a condom or get a blood test. I have had to change my thoughts on this. I have had to learn to have more respect and love for my life. I have had to learn that it's okay to ask tough questions. I have had to take more responsibility for how I feel about someone before sleeping with him. This has not been easy and sometimes I wish I didn't care, but I do. If I don't, I might contract a bothersome and expensive STD, possibly one that could result in a horrible and lonely death.

If you want to have sex with someone, talk about whether either of you is at risk for AIDS or other infections. Get tested together, if needed. Once you are in a relationship, practice safe sex habits. If you don't, you could give him or her a disease that could kill or cause a lifetime of health problems.

Birth Control and Pregnancy

Part of taking responsibility for sex involves deciding whether or not to use birth control. Birth control is the responsibility of both men and women. If you decide to use birth control, you need to decide what type to use. The most common are: pill, diaphragm, sponge, condom, or foam. There is also the rhythm method, but it is not as reliable as the other methods mentioned. If you decide not to use birth control, you need to think through how you would emotionally and financially manage a child at this time.

Marriage and Children

Don't rush into marriage after you leave the cult. You will feel lonely and overwhelmed at times and you will want the closeness of another person both physically and emotionally. But please remember you have been through a very difficult experience. Give yourself time to heal before you take on any new responsibilities. Get to know yourself again (or for the first time) before becoming too involved with another person. This will help you choose the best partner for you.

While you were in the cult you were not allowed to explore your own uniqueness. Residual suggestions of what is right for you as defined by the cult may still be a part of your thinking. If you make unalterable decisions too quickly right now, such as marriage and children, they may be the wrong decisions for you. Give yourself time, perhaps at least one year, before making any unalterable decisions.

Exercise-Sexual Behavior

List your concerns and fears about sex. Discuss these with someone you trust. What topics do you want more information about? Check your library for reliable books and articles on these topics. Also, consider discussing your questions with your doctor or health care practitioner.

Depression

Every ex-cultist I have known has experienced depression. It varies in length and intensity. Those who don't experience depression may be denying their feelings of sadness and hopelessness. Some types of depression require medication. If you cannot work through your depression, you might want to consider medication prescribed by a trained and competent psychiatrist. Be sure to eat right and get plenty of rest (see Appendix D.)

Deceived

There is no doubt about it, recognizing you were deceived, manipulated, and controlled is enraging. What a sense of being lied to and of being conned! What a sense of being deceived! For many, it is a sense of violation akin only to rape—the rape of the mind.

Cults don't stop with the mind, though. They rape your soul and your spirituality. They rape the very dreams that make you who you are. "What is it you would like in your life or in the world that isn't there now?" they ask. And we, innocent of the trap before us, told them our dreams, such as a world at peace, more love between people, harmony in the home, financial stability, inner peace, a meaningful job, a meaningful life.

We trusted them to show us the pathway. We gave up family, friends, careers, loved ones, educations, and more to follow a dream. The dream became a fog. When the fog cleared, we'd been had—big time. We'd lost a lot.

It takes time to grieve the loss of all these many things. Sometimes the pain of grieving can become so intense that people deny or repress the pain. They insist on "getting on with things" and tell themselves that everything is fine. Inevitably, the pain will need to be processed and this neglected wound will cry out for attention when least expected. It is helpful to moderate the pain so as not to become immobilized, but the pain still needs to be felt and the loss still needs to be grieved. This takes time and courage. It also takes permission from you and from your environment.

Blind Trust vs. Selective Trust

We lost family, friends, relationships, careers, educations, spouses, children, money and more money, property, health, and time, and we lost trust. We lost trust in our ability to make decisions, in religion, in government, in academia, in the media, in medicine, in business, and in the military.

You name it; we couldn't trust it. The cult had wedged that much fear into us. They alone had the truth; all else was lies. Some of that ideology haunts most of us, even after we leave, in the form of phobias, such as "you can't trust anyone...everyone's out to get you."

It's not true that you can't trust the government, but you can't *blindly* trust. You need to assess, evaluate, reason, deduce and decide what to trust about the government. The work of recovery is to move from the blind trust of the cult to trusting *selectively* after applying good decision-making skills. It's not true that you can't trust religion, business, medicine, or relationships. But you cannot blindly trust. You must learn to trust selectively.

Loss of Innocence

Is it any wonder that part of recovery involves being depressed and sad about these losses? Not just the loss of people, places and things, but also the loss of innocence. We can have blind faith no more. We know in a very real way that it is not safe. Nor can we have blind faith in reason or emotions. We must integrate them. We must listen to the feedback our feelings are giving us and not deny or rationalize it. We need to learn to evaluate what is going on between our hearts and our minds. We have to learn to listen to our thoughts and feelings and take responsibility for what is there.

Unable to Sleep

There was a period of about three months in the first year of recovery when I remember having great difficulty sleeping. I dreaded the end of the day. I would lie down to sleep and so many impressions of people and things would flood my mind. I would be so overwhelmed that I would cry for hours—a kind of crying I will never forget and have never had since then. It was a deep, gut-wrenching crying, as if I were going to vomit my guts. I cried for the people left behind, for the years I lost, for the family events missed, the boyfriends I never knew, and more.

Fortunately, there was an ex-cultist available to me on the phone in those painful late hours and we would talk about many of the issues I was trying to work through. I was also getting counseling. Those were some really tough months. Thank goodness for my friend on the phone. I keep thinking this grieving process is like a phoenix from the ashes, or as the old men sing in the movie "Chitty, Chitty, Bang, Bang"—up from the ashes grow the roses of success. I took inspiration from wherever I could find it and clung to it.

The Buddy System

If your cult was into "going through" or "experiencing" pain as a cleansing mechanism, feeling depression might be scary and loaded for you. I would suggest you go ahead and try to grieve the losses you've experienced. You can do this by using the "buddy system." Remember the buddy system from summer camp? You would team up in twos and keep an eye out for each other. You can team up in the healing process as well.

Don't swim in the pain alone. Talk your feelings over with a trusted friend or friends, other ex-cultists, and/or a therapist. Take your time. Grieving is a very important part of healing. To be a bit poetic, it's as if the tears are washing the wound clean so it can heal.

Spiritual Matters

Many ex-cultists are very confused, angry, and in pain about spiritual matters after their cult experience. They feel that God has let them down. The concept of a higher power was used against them to control and manipulate them. The lyrics of great old songs and hymns were rewritten with cult lyrics. Those songs now carry painful memories and the potential for floating. Even the feeling of a Bible in their lap can trigger sorrow. To embrace spiritual things again or too soon can be frightening and painful, even dangerous.

What the Cult Taught Me

For many ex-cultists, most of their knowledge of the Bible or other spiritual writings has come from the cult. Let me ask you a question, then, about the integrity of those teachings.

If the cult was so intent on manipulating you, if many of their activities and actions were deceitful and destructive, can you trust what they taught you about spiritual things? If you want to continue to believe their teachings, I suggest you take the time to separate out the wheat from the chaff. Take time after you're stronger to weed out the half-truths and coercive ideologies that aren't spiritually founded at all, but were taught in order to manipulate and control you.

It is very difficult to heal if you are divided between continuing the cult's teachings and trying to exit from its manipulative snares. Remember the snare is not just physical. They control followers with ideas and the ideas are communicated through the teachings.

Some ex-cultists are afraid to let go of their readings, meditations, tapes, etc. After you have listened to teachings and tapes for so many hours and for so many days and years, it's disorienting not to have them. For others, it's a great relief not to be chained to all those meetings and classes and teachings.

Try Taking a Breather

It was suggested to me by my deprogrammer to put the meditation and teachings aside for awhile. I suggest the same to you. You need to be actively engaging your mind in reality testing and critical thinking. If you want to, you can go back to the teachings later, when you're stronger. You also want to be careful not to create the "bang the bruise" effect.

You're already trying to process being used and deceived by the cult. That's a lot of stress. You can add to that stress by continuing to meditate and study the books the cult used. This won't help your recovery. You can also stir up memories that may cause floating and flashbacks.

It's okay to back off from meditation and religion for as long as you need in order to sort out your thoughts and feelings. You may find that you can never go back to the religion you once knew as a child. Some ex-cultists have been able to return, but I have not. However, I have found a close and nurturing relationship with God outside of formal religion. I realize some ex-cultists and clergy do not believe that God is available outside of religion.

I believe that life wants you to be healthy and whole. I believe this because it is inherent in all living things to heal. It's hard to heal when you're afraid and in pain. If religion makes you feel that way, avoid it until you are ready to work through your feelings. I bet that God understands what you're going through.

Religious Answers Now

If my advice does not seem right for you, if you feel that you must address religious issues now, talk to pastoral counselors. These are people who are trained in religion and in counseling. Talk to more than one for different points of view. You will find that God put shades of gray on the planet in ideas as well as nature. Be careful not to fall into the "hear-and-believe" mode of the cult. Ask questions and more questions. If the pastoral counselor does not like your questions, you can ask someone else until you get satisfactory answers. (See Bussell, 1983; Bussell, 1985; LeBar, 1989.)

Summary

It is important to take the time to learn about abusive groups and to work through the pain of the experience. Take the time, the discipline, and the courage to heal thoroughly. Don't repress your feelings—feel them and talk them out. Anger, depression, and a sense of being overwhelmed are very normal. In time, you will be able to sort through how you feel about spiritual matters. This work requires an environment that is nurturing and encourages independent decision-making. Be patient and gentle with yourself.

Chapter 3:
Phase Three–Rebuilding and Dreaming

*He has achieved success who has lived well, laughed
often and loved much.*
—Bessie Anderson Stanley

What do you do once the shock, grief, and pain have been talked out?
What do you do when you have studied mind control and yourself so
thoroughly you know why it won't happen to you again? What do you do
after you have reconnected with yourself, family, and friends? You build
or rebuild a life plan. This may include a career, education, intimate
relationship, family, community service, personal interests, and financial
stability.

Putting it in Perspective

A friend mentioned she was taking a workshop to learn how to make
wreaths. How insignificant it can seem to make a wreath, I thought,
when you've been spending the past several years trying to save the
world. How insignificant everything seems.

Fanaticism

Someone told me the toughest job for the ex-cultist is to learn what
normal is after having been a fanatic (all or nothing) for so long. I found
this to be very true. For a few years after I returned home, there was a
sense of urgency that plagued me. I assumed this urgency had been
burned into my nerves. For years the cult had drilled into me the
immediate, pending world doom I alone could alleviate by following
them.

It was hard to work when I returned home. In fact, I didn't for about a
year. The only marketable job skill I had was typing, so I eventually
worked as a secretary. Once the novelty of being back in the real world
wore off, depression set in. With that depression came a sense of
uselessness. I'd been so fanatically intent on saving the world that now
typing a letter seemed so trivial and insignificant.

It also seemed senseless to get excited about birthday parties, bridal and
baby showers, and other occasions. I found myself so uncomfortable at
these events. Couldn't everyone see how trivial they were? Didn't
everyone know that while they were busy enjoying cake and ice cream,
people were being hurt and abused by cults? Couldn't everyone see how

serious the condition of the world was? How could they be happy another child was born?

As time went by, I realized I needed these events not only to forget the troubles of the world for a few hours, but to help me put my problems within the perspective of life's continual renewal.

Life Regenerates and Evolves

While I was in the depths of depression and hopelessness, I went to the wedding of an ex-cultist with Brian and Steve, also ex-cultists. The wedding only made me feel more depressed. There was no one special in my life. Maybe, I thought, I had missed the man for me while in the cult. Maybe I'd be alone forever.

On the way home from the wedding, the three of us got to talking. Steve said something that really "clicked" for me and was the spark that helped me start out of the seemingly endless depression I had been in.

He talked of how civilization was evolving. That humanity was different now from what it was 100 years ago and would be different 100 years from now (Bucke, 1923). "Really?," I asked. "Do you really think people are learning and changing?" "Definitely," he replied. So I began to wonder. Are we as a people different for the struggles and tears of those who came before us? Have the accomplishments of others helped us to be a better people, a different people?

Making a Difference

I looked to nature for some insight about evolution. Nature certainly was changing, always adapting to its everchanging environment. But was life getting better? I looked back in history and pondered the development of modern medicine, agriculture, mental health, and more. Certainly, the child labor laws no longer allowed children to be abused in industry as they were in the sweatshops of years ago.

It seemed that humanity was capable of many achievements along the continuum between good and evil. It became quite clear as I kept thinking about it, that people could change. Some people anyway. Enough people could change, I thought, to make the effort of my life worthwhile. I couldn't save the world anymore, but my life could still make a difference. I realized that there was a reason to face the struggle of recovery and stick with it other than my own gratification. There was a reason to try to put the pieces of my life back together in a healthier way. My life could make a difference.

I realized, however, that to make a difference would require many different kinds of skills. I would have to learn to use the skills I did have and acquire the skills I didn't have. What good would it be if I was very good at something, but nobody was listening to me?

Exercise–Skills and Strengths

List at least five of your strengths or skills (example: organized, artistic). How could these skills and strengths be used to make your community a better place?

Expectations

Making a difference almost always involves more than being competent at something. It involves learning how to communicate with others in such a way that they can hear you. Too often ex-cultists have expectations of others that are unrealistic.

Many ex-cultists have great ideas of how they can use the skills and experiences they acquired while in the cult to make a difference in their communities. But having lived in an all-or-nothing world, they often have severely distorted expectations about how others should respond to their ideas. If they were leaders in their cults, they were probably used to people responding with total acceptance and obedience. Ex-cultists often still expect all or nothing from others. This attitude naturally makes people defensive and angry.

Before trying to communicate with others, it is helpful to ask "what kinds of expectations can I have of this listener? Where are these expectations on the gray scale? Am I still in the all-or-nothing, totalistic mind set?" It's important to learn to recognize the expectations you have of yourself and of others and to test how realistic these expectations are.

Interact with Others

Often ex-cultists get stuck in the fear of being hurt again and try to protect themselves by minimizing any interaction with others. They stay huddled in their apartments. This is okay for a while. But, if you're one of these people, perhaps you can challenge yourself to grow and change. In time, try to begin to work toward changing the expectations you have of how others should respond to you by interacting with people and seeing what does and doesn't work. Don't worry if you make mistakes. Everyone does.

Work at dismantling the all-or-nothing mind set the cult taught you. Look for the subtle and hidden signals of this kind of thinking. For some, this can be particularly difficult since all-or-nothing thinking will seem normal to the pre-cult self.

Exercise–Expectations

Think of a friend, family member, or coworker with whom you get frustrated or angry. Write down your expectations of this person—why it is they make you upset. Review the expectations and ask yourself where each expectation is on the gray scale. How could you adjust your expectations? Discuss this adjustment process with others. Do your expectations sound reasonable to them? If so, why? If not, adjust your expectations again. Try interacting with the adjusted expectations. What happened? Why?

Becoming Your Own Coach

One of the best things you can ever do for yourself is to become you own best friend and coach, if you aren't already. We all need to be believed in and we all need a little inspiration and coaching now and then.

Isn't it grand to genuinely respect yourself for the person you are and to feel proud of your accomplishments! You are someone special. You have something to give. You got knocked down hard but you're getting back up on your feet slowly but surely. You're making mistakes, but you're learning from them. You get tired and scared, lonely and confused, but you don't quit. You learn how to do some things well and share that knowledge and encouragement with others. That's something to be proud of and to feel good about.

"Steady at the helm, lass," I tell myself when a situation gets a little panicky. That's a sailor's expression. The helm steers the ship through wind, rain, and dark of night. "Steady, and keep your wits about you, now." Sometimes you need to coach yourself through the rough spots. You need to believe in you.

Learning New Skills

When I realized I could learn new skills, new possibilities opened up to me. I had to realize, though, that acquiring new skills meant I would be changing. Change can be hard for some people. "For many people," as Alfred Adler said, "the solution is more frightening than the problem."

Change usually leads to growth. For some it's an adventure, a door to new freedoms and experiences. For others, change is very threatening. Change means letting go of an old way and moving onto a different place. This takes time and courage.

"Growth has not only rewards and pleasure, but also many intrinsic pains and always will have. Each step forward is a step into the unfamiliar and is thought of as possibly dangerous. It also frequently means giving up something familiar and good and satisfying. It frequently means a parting and a separation with consequent nostalgia, loneliness, and mourning. It also often means giving up a simpler and easier and less effortful life in exchange for a more demanding, more difficult life. Growth forward is in spite of these losses and therefore requires courage, strength in the individual, as well as protection, permission, and encouragement from the environment, especially for the child." (A.H. Maslow, "Some Basic Propositions of Holistic-Dynamic Psychology," an unpublished paper, Brandeis University.)

Taking Inventory

What if you feel like a complete jerk, a failure? "Everytime I get up, something knocks me down." Well, if you keep tripping, get new shoelaces. What I mean is, acquire new skills and/or improve others. Change. We often keep making mistakes because we aren't hearing and integrating feedback from our emotions and our reason. Identify the areas of your thinking and feelings that need improvement.

Exercise–Self-Assessment

Try asking yourself the following questions and writing down the answers: What activities can I do well? What skills do I have? Which feelings can I hear well? Which thinking faculties are strong (for example, listening, assessment, perception, reason)? What are my strengths at work? With friends? At school? At home? What areas need improvement? How could I improve these areas? Give details and timeframes.

Remember, you are worth the effort. You can learn to make good decisions. Stick with it. You can do it.

Hang in there! Remember, "steady as she goes."

Going Back to School

To learn new skills, test expectations, and stimulate the mind try going back to school. I went back to finish my B.A. I looked around for something at night that I could afford and someone suggested Harvard's Extension University. "Who, me? At Harvard? You've got to be kidding!" But when I found it cost less than other local colleges, I decided to bite the bullet. Five years later, I walked through The Yard in my graduation gown laughing at the cult and awfully darn proud of me.

The most wonderful thing happened to me there, I rediscovered the wonder and excitement of learning and of thinking. It was very stimulating and very hard, but it was the best thing I have ever done for myself, not only as an ex-cultist but also as a woman.

There are many local adult education courses offered these days, many for credit toward a degree. If you decide to give it a try, I suggest that the first class or two be on a subject that really turns you on. Try not to get bogged down in the "shoulds." Let the first class be just for fun.

Because so many of us have lost so much time while in the cult, the temptation is to jump right into trying to catch up. But, I'd really like to suggest that the first course be just for fun—sort of "rev the engines." There is such a sense of hopelessness that can drag you down during recovery that it can be very healing to get excited about "Brazilian Rainforests," "Quantum Mechanics," "Bill Shakespeare" or whatever subject turns you on. (Those in support positions to the ex-cultist need to back off with the "shoulds" here.)

Exercise–Learning Assessment

Think about a time when you had a lot of fun learning something. What did you learn? How did you learn it? What made it fun? Think about a painful learning experience. What did you learn? How did you (have to) learn it? What made it painful? Write down what makes learning fun for you. How can you structure future learning events so they are fun?

Learning Styles

Recently, I've learned something really quite interesting while at work. It is that different people have different styles or orientations toward learning. Some people are more abstract and conceptual as learners. Others are more concrete and analytical. Some ask "why?" while others more often approach with "how?" Still others ask "if, then?" and some ask "what?".

Not everyone learns in the same way. Unfortunately, our school systems and textbooks are designed to accommodate only a couple of the many learning styles. That's why some people had such a hard time in school despite being smart. If you were one of those people, check out the library or a legitimate evaluation program to learn how to structure the learning process to better fit with your style.

If you suspect you might have a learning disability, such as dyslexia, remedial help is available. Check with your health care provider or state agency for more information on where to get testing and help. If testing is a loaded issue for you, use the buddy system (see The Buddy System).

Exercise-Learning Styles

If you are learning in a group situation, how does your learning style add to the group learning experience? How does it complement other learning styles? How might it clash with other learning styles? (Example: in learning a new card game, some people do well to sit quietly and read about the game thoroughly before playing. Others prefer to watch someone else play first. Others prefer to start playing and learn as they go.)

Decision-Making

A key skill to learn for life is how to make a good decision. How do you figure out what action to take or not to take in any given situation? If God or whoever is not providing you with the answer and if the cult leader(s) is not telling you what to do, how do you figure out what's the best thing to do?

Resources

You make decisions based on information from resources. Those resources should include your own knowledge and reasoning as well as other sources. To make a sound decision you need to determine if you have enough information and if that information comes from valid sources. Sometimes checking resources involves a lot of work.

Had I checked out the cult more thoroughly, I would have turned and walked away at the first encounter. I wouldn't have listened. I suspect if someone had told you the cult used sophisticated psychological controls you would not have listened further either. But digging out information and thinking it through takes time and effort and most people do not do it very well.

Impulsive Decisions

Most people are impulsive decision makers not well-reasoned or well-thought-out decision makers. Impulsive decision-making is encouraged by the media, advertisers, and many salespeople. We are inundated with the message "do it now and be acceptable." Well, you can say "no" now. You can say "I want to go away and think it over, talk it over with someone more knowledgeable."

Some ex-cultists go through great anguish at first trying to make decisions. For years, someone else has guided them and told them what to think, say, eat, and do. Afterwards, even choosing a tube of toothpaste can be embarrassingly confusing and debilitating. You can use any decision to develop, regain, and practice good thorough decision-making skills.

An Example–Buying Toothpaste

Let's use the toothpaste as an example of how to think something through. Use who, what, when, where, why, and how (remember these from Phase One?). Here are some steps:

1. First, clarify why you're doing something. Buying toothpaste for a diabetic friend will be different, probably, from buying it for yourself.

2. Second, determine the decision-making criteria by asking questions, such as:
   - How much to buy?
   - What color should it be?
   - Should it be in environmentally friendly packaging?
   - Should it be in a screw top or push button container?
   - What should the ingredients contain or not contain?
   - How much to spend?
   - Does the person have a favorite brand or would they like to try something new?

3. Third, make a decision. You may only be able to narrow the choices down and start the process over again. Or you may have enough information to decide. If you are having trouble deciding, don't let someone push you into a decision. Take your time, stay with it, and you will be able to figure out what to do, even if it is to toss a coin.

4. Fourth, once you have decided, go for it. You might need a plan to go purchase it, but you can figure that out, too. If at first you feel overwhelmed, break the process up into small chunks, such as:
   - Pull out the money
   - Choose the store
   - Go to the store
   - Purchase the product
   - Return home
   - Wrap the gift
   - Take the gift to your friend

5. Fifth, if your decision turns out to be a mistake, learn from it. Don't beat yourself up for it. When your decisions are right, be sure to congratulate yourself. Stay focused on learning, not being right.

Little Decisions to Big Decisions

Now, this might sound a bit ridiculous to some people, but I have known ex-cultists who were kept in isolation most of their ten plus years of involvement. Going out the door into "the world" to buy a gift for someone was an overwhelming and frightening experience. What I'm trying to demonstrate here is not how to make buying toothpaste as complicated as possible, but that you can teach yourself how to make good decisions. Take a little decision and use it to understand the steps that went into the process of decision-making.

What if you are faced with a big decision, such as how to rewrite your résumé, which major to choose in college, to sue the cult, or whether to date or marry a particular person? If you have developed good decision-making skills and have practiced making good decisions, you can face these bigger questions with a sense of competence.

So, try using little decisions to help yourself understand the decision-making process. Take the time to check your resources. Once you have made a decision, discuss it with others, "bounce" it off them. This is called *reality testing*. Does this decision make sense to others, too? Once you have decided to test the waters, go ahead and do it. Don't worry if you make a few errors. You can learn to make competent choices and, thereby, manage your life.

Exercise–Decision-Making

Write down something you need to do or buy or would like to do or buy. Now, clarify. Exactly what do you need to have done by when and for whom? List the information (criteria) you need in order to make a good decision. Decide what to do. Do it.

Letting Go of Myths

Learning how to trust selectively without losing hope in life is part of the process of maturing or growing up. Within the process of separating from the dependent status of children and moving into the independent then interdependent state of adulthood is the process of letting go.

Part of this letting go involves letting go of myths and dependencies. Blind trust is a form of dependency, and it is not healthy. When many of us were young, blind trust and obedience was an easier way to face the complexities of the world and/or such trust was demanded by parents or religion. The time comes, however, to let blind trust go and learn how to trust selectively based on good evaluation skills.

A Smidgen of Truth

The cult taught many myths. Part of what makes recovering from a cult experience so very difficult and why I said it takes time, mental discipline, and courage is that each part of these myths has some small kernel of truth to it. But the truth is gnarled into the myths as the roots of grass are gnarled into the dirt. Separating the lie from reality can be subtle and hard work. Unless one works through the recovery process, these myths will remain intermingled in the mind and continue to distort reality for years.

Goodbye Myths, Hello Responsibility

To let go of a myth is to change yourself. For example, if you stop believing the myth that your lover is the right person for you in all ways, then you have to figure out what to do when your lover is not enough. You will need to develop other supportive relationships with people. There is a risk associated with this. There may be interpersonal skills you will need to develop. There is work that follows the letting go of a myth. And there is the sorrow and grief of losing the myth.

In order to heal and feel safe, I have had to discard many myths. Myths about what friendship should be, what God should be, what love should be (this is really a tough one), what a relationship should be, what a boss should be, what a job should be, what anything should be. I know letting go of myths is part of growing up and I realize it's necessary to healing, but it's still very hard to do. It is hard to accept that there are no easy answers in a society addicted to quick fixes.

Shortcuts and Distortions

Life can be very complex and myths can provide shortcuts to processing information. When these myths or ideas are exploited by abusive groups or the media, they have the power to distort expectations and manipulate behavior in very subtle ways (Cialdini, 1984). When people rely on the shortcut and stop thinking about what a myth really means or how it affects us, this can hide problems.

Our culture is drowning in myths. Myths are buried deep in our songs and rituals reinforced by well-meaning but not critically thinking families and friends. It's very scary for an ex-cultist, who has been manipulated, raped, and robbed by subtle and unquestioned ideas, to emerge from the cult experience into a society which is manipulated by subtle and unquestioned ideas.

It's nerve-wracking to try to develop friendships and support systems with people who cannot see how they are being manipulated by images and ideas around them, when it was this same lack of awareness of manipulative systems that enabled us to be conned into a cult which later almost destroyed us, certainly robbed us.

Untangling and Evaluating

It takes work and more work to untangle these "grassroots" as I call them, these intertwined half-truths which permeate our culture and permeated the cult. But when you carefully evaluate an idea and determine how, if, and to what extent it applies to you, and then build it into your picture of life, you end up with a stronger sense of who you are. You can find you are more at peace within yourself and with the world around you.

As I mentioned, this takes mental discipline and work. Once you get the hang of critical thinking, the payoffs in better decision-making and self-confidence are great!

Exercise–A Culture of Myths

What are some myths you see and hear around you? Watch TV or listen to the radio for fifteen minutes and write down the myths you can find. Discuss these with a friend. To evaluate a myth or idea, try the following:

1. *Identify the idea or myth you want to question.*
2. *Assess, evaluate, and critique it keeping in mind what's right for you.*
3. *Modify, integrate, apply, and test it within your life.*

When you get really good at myth detection, you will be amazed at how many myths you hear. One of the most prevalent myths today is "you can have it all." Why is this not true? Why is it dangerous to perpetuate some myths? What kinds of problems can you predict because of how this myth is shaping people's expectations today?

Summary

There are so many wonderful aspects to life. You are free now to learn of them and to enjoy them. You are free to take the risks and enjoy the fruits of your efforts. With this freedom comes the responsibility and accountability for your actions. Learn the skills that can take you where you want to go with your life and change the habits that get in your way.

Be your own best friend and coach. (See Newman and Berkowitz, 1971.)

Chapter 4:
The Role of the Family

*A life is beautiful and ideal, or the reverse, only when
we have taken into our consideration the social as well
as the family relationship.*
—Havelock Ellis

In the previous chapters, I have written to ex-cultists. In this chapter I
hope to help ex-cultists by speaking to their families and those in a
supportive role. (See Ross and Langone, 1988.) For additional excellent
information, please review the Reference List. Much of the information
in this chapter with some modifications will also be of great help to a
spouse whose partner is involved with an excessive group.

The family is usually greatly relieved to have their loved one home. It's
an adjustment for everyone. Months, often years, of anguish and fear
are over. As in the return of the prodigal child, it is a time of great joy.

Not all families are fortunate enough to see the return of their loved
one(s). The group may have isolated the loved one to an unknown place
where no contact is allowed. Some families continue indefinitely to send
letters knowing the letters are screened by the group's leaders. Most
families learn early not to send money, as it is usually turned over to the
group. These families can often benefit from professional counseling to
help them cope with their frustration and despair.

Those families whose member leaves the group can be a source of great
support and encouragement. Through the ups and downs of recovery,
the family can be there with love and understanding, to listen and
empathize. Years of strained communication can melt away as new
memories of love and laughter replace the years of frustration and
anguish.

Pointers

Here are a few pointers which can help families provide a nurturing
environment that simultaneously encourages independence:

- Recognize that recovery can take years. Some damage may be
  irreparable.
- Understand, accept, and grieve your own lost time and lost
  experiences with loved ones.
- Don't be confrontational. Give the loved one time to let go of his
  or her loyalty to the group and its leaders and to acknowledge the
  deception.

- Do not try to overprotect or control the loved one. Learn to negotiate.

- Forgive your loved one for the pain he caused you while in the cult, and *tell* him that you forgive him.

- Encourage independent decision-making.

- Recognize the loved one may need financial support during recovery, but that financial and emotional independence should be encouraged.

- Accept and respect the accomplishments the loved one made while in the cult.

- Understand the loved one's often intense aversion to authority figures.

Patient and Hopeful

Some of you have tried to reach your child and the intervention failed. There may be little contact left between you now. Some of you have discovered that your child has left the state or country and you have no idea where he or she is. Everyday you live not knowing if your child is alive or dead, healthy or injured. What happiness there may be for your child, you know is false. You may have been left with cosigned loans or other bills. You feel hurt, abandoned, angry, confused, and inept at reaching the one you love and helping him or her. Somehow, you go on.

Whatever contact you do have, keep it as upbeat as possible. Should your child leave someday, the fewer barriers there are to returning to you the better. Unlike other walkaways who leave the group and remained confused and plagued with fears, if your child comes home, you can make sure he gets adequate medical and theraputic attention.

As painful as it is, you need to embrace the possibility that your child may never come home. You may never know if he marries, has children, is successful at his work, or falls ill. You have been abandoned. You must grieve this terrible loss and go on with your life. You need to let go of this "lost child" in order to cope with the everyday demands on your family and on your life. Remember as best you can that it is the cult that has done this to you and your family, not the cultist.

Exercise–For the Future

By the time your child returns home, your heart may have long forgotten who he was—the talents, joys, likes and dislikes that made him who he was. He will need you to help him remember. If it's not too painful, try writing down now all you can remember of him the way he was before the cult. Allow yourself to hurt and to cry. Tuck it away with a prayer.

Time Lost Forever

Parents have dreams for their child and envision sharing time and love with him as the years go by. For many families of ex-cultists, parents and siblings alike, a gap of lost years with their loved one exists.

Families can be caught in a tricky position. In the same way that an ex-cultist wants to reclaim those lost years and the moments that could have been, so the family wants to reclaim those lost moments, too. The cult stole time, love, and laughter not only from the ex-cultist, but from the ex-cultist's family as well. This is a real loss that should be grieved.

If the family is unconsciously asking to recapture those lost years, this puts too much pressure on the ex-cultist, and it is unrealistic. Whether you are a parent or stepparent who had a child or grandchild in the cult, a child who had a parent or grandparent in a cult, a sibling or friend, it is important to realize that it's okay to want to recapture those lost moments, but you can't.

Let go, grieve the loss, and start anew.

Exercise–What I Wanted for You

List four goals not yet realized that you wanted for your child. By what age would your child have accomplished each goal? Given what you know now, is each goal still appropriate? Write down how the cult experience has affected the reaching of each goal for your child. How has the cult experience helped? Grieve the loss or delay of any of these goals.

What would be the advantage of discussing this exercise with your loved one? What does your child think about these goals? To what extent are your goals motivated by concern and respect and to what extent are they motivated by a desire to control? Can you let go of inappropriate goals?

Accept the Changes

It's hard when a friend or family member who was close to you now is physically and emotionally distant. He is alone with his pain and you can't reach him. It can help to realize that like a veteran returning from a war, he has been somewhere you have not been, exposed to horrors of a trauma you can only imagine. For all your years of experience, you have not been in his war. You did not lose the time, friends, and dreams that he lost. But you still lost something.

You lost your loved one the way he used to be. He is back, but he will never be who he was. Healing will mean integrating the pain he has known. This will change him. It should change you, too. You and your family can demonstrate your love by accepting the changes this experience has caused. This may mean letting go of what you wanted him to be.

Integration Takes Time

Some of those years included key developmental periods for both the loved one and the family. Events, which would have helped the family let go of the loved one and the loved one let go of the family, did not happen. Because of this, both family and loved one can be stunted or "on hold" developmentally in some key ways.

On the other hand, ex-cultists have been exposed to experiences that have matured them beyond their years, such as leadership responsibilities and sexual activity. The very reality of having been ideologically and psychologically raped has catapulted ex-cultists to a developmental space inconsistent with their years.

This mismatch of years and experiences takes very hard work to integrate into a unified whole. Let it take time.

Exercise–Expectations

Write down all the expectations you have of your loved one for the first year of recovery. Now, write down all your expectations for the second and third years of recovery. Discuss these expectations with a friend who has been traumatized and recovered or someone knowledgeable about trauma. How realistic are your expectations? Modify your expectations and review them with your friend.

Missed Events

Some ex-cultists, because of the constraints of the cult, missed critical life events with their families and friends, such as births, deaths, marriages, religious observances, and graduations. Even though ex-cultists are not fully responsible for not having attended these events, it helps to hear that they have been forgiven. Discuss it with them. Let them know you still love and respect them and that you understand it was the cult that kept them from sharing these key family events. They also need to forgive themselves. Both the families and ex-cultists need to grieve the loss of not having shared these events.

Basic Skills

Also lost to the ex-cultists were the opportunities to develop basic self-management skills, such as:

1. Finding an apartment. These skills might include:
    a. Arranging for gas, oil, electricity, phone, water
    b. Interviewing and contracting with a landlord
    c. Managing neighbor and roommate conflicts
2. Finding transportation. These skills might include:
    a. Deciphering bus, subway, and train schedules
    b. Getting a driver's license
    c. Buying and maintaining a vehicle
    d. Processing an insurance application or claim
    e. Processing registration and excise tax forms
3. Finding a job. These skills might include:
    a. Writing a résumé
    b. Arranging for initial and follow-up job interviews
    c. Interviewing skills
    d. Appropriate work clothes, expectations, and behaviors
4. Finding health care. These skills might include:
    a. Assessing a doctor, specialist, and dentist
    b. Setting up initial and follow-up appointments
    c. Getting regular exams
    d. Processing an insurance application and claim form
    e. Taking medication
    f. Learning and practicing good dental, nutritional, and exercise habits
5. Managing money. These skills might include:
    a. Setting up a budget
    b. Opening a savings and checking account
    c. Reconciling bank statements
    d. Paying bills
    e. Establishing credit

It may be very painful for you to see your forty-year-old family member overwhelmed, even immobilized, at the idea of a doctor's appointment, getting an apartment, or opening a checking account. The questions may seem so basic to you, but remember he has been in another world for a long time.

You can help with this potentially overwhelming array of basic skills. Take the time to teach the necessary skills without judging or criticizing.

Teach with patience, humor, and encouragement. Avoid being controlling or overprotective and encourage self-reliance.

Respecting Their Accomplishments

When I was deprogrammed in 1980, the theory was that to let the loved one admit anything good could come out of the cult experience was to encourage them to return. Those who work with ex-cultists have since realized that this theory was wrong. *Ex-cultists need to be able to take the good with them from their experience.* There may not have been much of it, but there was some, and the ex-cultist is entitled to it.

Like many other ex-cultists, I was exposed to people, places, skills, and ideas in the cult that I probably would not have known otherwise. I learned many things, such as how to survive on $20 a month spending money, how to sleep in a semi with an overactive wet-nosed dog, how to run large meetings, survive in the wilderness, shoot firearms, work long hours, and jog ten miles. For every good experience, there were hours and hours of verbal and psychological abuse, but there were still some skills and experiences worth keeping.

Nieces, Nephews, and Grandchildren

Many ex-cultists were married in the cult and had children. Whether or not one is under mind control, being in a marriage and raising children is an accomplishment. These ex-cultists have their own families and responsibilities to those families. How they choose to handle those responsibilities during the trauma of exiting and recovery may or may not be to your liking. But your support is needed. You can be most effective as a sounding board:

- Listening
- Gently raising questions
- Offering advice, if requested
- Being supportive

Remember, ex-cultists need to learn to make their own decisions and to carry them out. Nieces, nephews, and grandchildren will survive these difficult months and years better, if the extended family is supportive and non-argumentative.

Covered in Bruises

A visual aid that might help is to imagine your loved one covered with dark bruises. Remember, the pain is psychological and may not be visible on the outside, but the wounds can run very deep. Will it help to add pressure to these bruises or to step back and simply be there? As ex-cultists relearn how to use their badly bruised mental faculties and reconnect with long frozen emotions, will it help to do the tasks for them or to encourage and applaud them? You may not feel as if applause is much of a contribution, but it is!

Honor what they have accomplished while they were in the cult and give them space to work out their new challenges in their own way and in their own time. Recovery can take years.

Will My Loved One Go Back to the Cult?

After escaping from one deprogramming, all my mother wanted to know the second time around was "will Wendy go back again?" She had read about "floating." She knew that even after all the work to get me out of the cult's clutches, I could float and go back again. (See Floating, p. 36.)

Family members should be aware that abusive groups use powerful psychological controls on their followers. The longer these controls are in place, the more difficult it may be for ex-cultists to regain a hold on their pre-cult identity. Certain stressors, such as cult language, phone calls from cultists, and meditation, can cause a floating experience. Ex-cultists may appear glassy-eyed, nonemotional or agitated, or disoriented. Usually, simply being aware that this phenomenon can occur, and encouraging ex-cultists to talk about what they are feeling or thinking, can defuse a floating situation.

Encourage Open Communication

The loved one won't talk, though, if the environment does not encourage open discussion. The ex-cultist is highly sensitized to being told what to do and how to think, even if it is done subtly. Demonstrate from the first moment the loved one is home that it's safe to talk here by listening. Don't judge, don't interrupt, offer opinions or advice, unless it is asked for. Just listen.

Questions as Mental Exercise

When you ask the ex-cultist a question, do not interrupt the answer. Focusing on a question, formulating the answer, and articulating the answer while responding to your non-verbal or verbal ('ah,' 'um') cues may still be difficult for your loved one. Let the loved one *exercise* his mental skills by completing this process from beginning (your question) to end (stating his answer). If the loved one gets lost and stalls, help him by restating the question. The exercise of thinking can be as important as or more important than the answer.

Do ask questions about things you don't understand. If the loved one cannot explain it to your satisfaction, don't push. Give him time. Maybe offer to help him study that particular question.

As you interact in a non-threatening and nurturing way, you are building a bridge for ex-cultists from the world they left behind to a new place. The stronger this bridge is to the new world, the easier the transition is away from the old one. You are competing with an illusion of total acceptance and total love. You have one thing the illusion doesn't have, though. You have integrity.

Exercise–Helping Behaviors

Ask the loved one if your behavior is helpful. Ask what you could do differently. Ask for their help in monitoring the changing of behaviors.

Eggshells and Frustration

You are going to get frustrated and feel inept. Hear me again. You are going to get very frustrated and feel inept. You are going to feel as if you're walking on eggshells. Sometimes the loved one will be sullen, sometimes he will explode for no apparent reason. Or, as my parents did, you will go into her room in the middle of the night and find her soaked with tears. You will hurt for him and get very angry at those who have caused your child so much pain. Sometimes you may want to get argumentative, but don't.

I can promise you, a healthy recovery will take longer than you expect.

Good news, though, to help you through those trying times. There are support groups for family members, too. The Cult Awareness Network (CAN) has been helping families for a long time. There may be a local chapter near you. If a CAN support group is not near you, consider a church support group, or a trauma or rape support group for families. The issues are often very similar, and you need support systems, too.

My Loved One Was Fooled

Yes, he was. That may be embarrassing for you. It is embarrassing for him, too. He was fooled, and it cost both of you. Is he still credible? If he got tricked once, won't he get tricked again? You ask that question of him and he responds with a hearty "no way."

Still, you're not sure. He's been home several months now, but you decide to keep an eye on him for awhile longer. "It's for his own good," you tell yourself. How do you think your adult loved one feels knowing you're doing this?

A Critical Difference

You have made poor choices, but you managed to spring back. Why? Because you had something you're assuming the ex-cultist had, but did not. This missing piece is the reason you could spring back after being tricked and he could not. You had the freedom to reason. Your loved one did not. As bizarre as this may sound, unbeknownst to your loved one, inhibitors were placed in his mind which prevented the mind from reasoning. These inhibitors were reinforced by the cult's teachings and activities. Without the ability to reason, he could not leave.

You may have a hard time grasping this because it stands in stark contrast to the myth of America, the Land of the Free, and our macho images of John Wayne and George Patton. But the cults have managed to capitalize on the human condition and on the limitations of our socialization processes. The cults have developed a methodology that can control people remotely. It's scary, but it's manageable.

Know the Force

If you are embarrassed by your loved one's involvement in a cult, you need to understand the power of these psychological forces better. Once you do, you won't be embarrassed, but you will be accepting, forgiving, and supportive. You won't doubt his credibility because you will understand the forces that controlled him. Now that those forces are being dismantled, the loved one's autonomy and self-direction are returning. He has credibility.

To understand mind control is to recognize your own vulnerability. For many weak parents, accepting their own vulnerability is too frightening. They cling to their myths of power and control, insisting that their child could have and should have known better than to get involved with the cult. They see this experience as a weakness in their child, instead of a reality of the human condition. They alienate their child and load a difficult recovery process with unnecessary guilt and shame. Don't be one of these parents!!

Exercise–Helping Assessment

List the sensitivities (major bruises) of your loved one. List the strengths and skills you have that could be helpful to a trauma victim (example: patient, good listener). List the tendencies you have that would alienate somone from trusting you and coming to you for help (example: overbearing, unpredictable). Discuss this with a trusted and honest friend. Discuss this with siblings or friends of the ex-cultist, if appropriate.

Speaking Out about Their Experience

Some loved ones want to talk and write about their experiences publicly, others do not. Some lecture during the first few years and then decide to move on to other responsibilities. Some lecture later on, some never do. This is a private decision for loved ones to make. Whether loved ones do or do not want to talk in public, their decision should be respected.

Not Ready

Unfortunately, there are well-meaning persons who try to "encourage" the ex-cultist to talk about his experience before he is ready to talk. And, as incredible as it may seem, some people try to pressure or "encourage" the ex-cultist to talk even if he does not want to. Does this sound like coercion to you? It should. How do you think it sounds to the ex-cultist? Are you pushing buttons and jeopardizing recovery? You might be.

Talking in public can be very validating, but if a loved one is not ready and not stable, he could float. He could also have some very serious problems in developing trusting relationships again. When the people he has come home to are acting the same way the cult did—coercing certain behaviors—it sets off buttons and generates fear, even terror.

As a parent or support person, don't let anyone, even an anti-cult advocate or clergy, push you into "encouraging" the ex-cultist to talk about something he is not ready to discuss. Talking about the experience at home is not the same as talking about it publicly.

What to Do About Religion?

Don't let the clergy of the religion your loved one used to follow push him into recommitting to that faith. You need to accept that your loved one may never go back to that faith. It may be too loaded for him. Clergy need to accept this, too.

I realize this can be an extremely difficult issue for some families; however, giving the ex-cultist a lot of time, even years to work out his thoughts and feelings, is important. I have known some ex-cultists who did choose to go back to their former faith. Some returned fairly quickly, some did not return for years.

As for myself, I remember sitting in my room and discussing my confusion about church and religion with God that first year I was home. I loved God and nothing could take that truth away. But how I chose to express that love and service was not going to be dictated to me again. I knew that God was big enough to touch my life without the religion I had once known. I asked God to honor my pain, to accept my weaknesses, and to forgive me for not returning to the church of my youth. I promised God I would love generously and with wisdom and that I would always do the best I could with my life. I have kept that promise.

This issue can be a true test of faith for a family and their religion. I only want to offer the thought that you need to let go and trust God to work in your loved one's life and not to push this issue, especially with a bruised and hurt loved one. God can work in his or her life without the formalities of religion.

Summary

You can be a critical part of a speedy and healthy recovery by providing an accepting and nurturing environment. Healing will take a lot of time. Do not control or be overprotective. Let go of the times together that were stolen from you and grieve your loss. Trust that in time with the right support and information your loved one can move on with life.

Epilogue

I hope this handbook has been of some help to you and your family and friends. It has meant a lot to me to share my struggles with you. Mine has been a very long and often extremely difficult journey. Learning to trust again takes lots of practice.

I hope you will keep at the process of recovery, continuing to heal and grow into the person you want to become. *Don't ever give up!* Take a breather now and then as needed, but continue to focus on what values and goals are important to you. And, please don't get too discouraged. There is beauty all around and your life can still make a difference in this world. Let the beauty and mystery of Life inspire and soothe you.

Work on setting realistic expectations of yourself and of others. This can be very hard to do. Keep testing expectations. Each person and situation is different. Have you reviewed your expectations of a particular person for a particular situation? If you are frustrated too often, the cause may be an overlooked unrealistic expectation or a hidden myth.

Keep a lookout for any subtle, residual thought-control cobwebs. Consider reworking the materials on some sort of regular basis for several years. Residual controls and influences can be hard to ferret out.

Good luck and best wishes for a healthy and fulfilling life. You have so much to offer. I will be cheering for you.

Appendix A:
Recommended Reading List

Here are some suggested readings on cults and other topics. You may want to think about, and discuss with others, how to personalize your recovery plan to your specific needs. Study questions and their answers for some of the readings listed under *Recovery 101* can be found in Appendix B and C. Please review the *Additional Readings* list for other materials that may interest you.

Recovery 101 – The Basics

"Coming Out of the Cults" (Singer,)1979
"Kids 'n' Cults" (Swope, 1980)
"Resisting Mind Control"(Andersen and Zimbardo, 1980)
✓ *Combatting Cult Mind Control* (Hassan, 1988)
Recovery from Cults (Langone, (Ed.), 1993).
✓*Thought Reform and the Psychology of Totalism*, Chapters 5, 12, 22 (Lifton, 1961)
✓*Touchstones* (Stoner and Kisser, 1992)
Trauma and Recovery (Herman, 1992)
Youth, Brainwashing and the Extremist Cults (Enroth, 1977)

Recovery 201 – Filling in the Gaps

The Disowned Self (Branden, 1971)
Global Politics (Ray, 1983)
✓*Influence* (Cialdini, 1984)
Moonwebs (Freed, 1980)
Transitions (Bridges, 1980)
The Worldly Philosophers (Heilbroner, 1980)

Recovery 301 – Additional Studies

The Politics of International Economic Relations (Spero, 1985)
The Feminine Mystique (Freidan, 1963)
Cults and Consequences (Andres and Lane, 1988)
The Amazing Brain (Ornstein and Thompson, 1984)
Healing the Child Within (Whitfield, 1987)
Passages (Sheehy, 1976)
The Road Less Traveled (Peck, 1978)

Appendix B:
Study Questions

Note that some of these materials were written about young people, when most of the people recruited and having left cults were young. The cults now include all age groups. Much of this material is still applicable and to all ages.

Please remember these questions and answers are simply a learning aid. This is not a test to determine your worth. Become aware of any all-or-nothing reactions you may have to this learning process and adjust such expectations.

"Coming Out of the Cults" (Singer, 1979)

1. Why did Singer and Miller conduct discussion groups?
2. When did participants report they joined cults?
3. What are the thirteen difficulties Singer describes that can affect people who leave a cult?
4. How does this information pertain to you?

Youth, Brainwashing and the Extremist Cults, Chapter 8 (Enroth, 1977)

1. More than anything else, what are the young people who pursue cults today involved in?
2. What are the eight elements Enroth outlines that lead to the transformation of personality and thinking?
3. How does this information pertain to you?

"Kids 'n' Cults" (Swope, 1980)

1. What are the three interwoven concepts of utopian literature in Europe and the American colonies?
2. What was the shocking conclusion Swope came to after meeting with 125 young adults from different cults?
3. What are the six characteristics of the people who join cults?
4. How many characteristics need to be present for recruitment to be effective?
5. What is the key to being recruited?
6. How does this information pertain to you?

Influence (Cialdini, 1984)

1. When are we most likely to accept the actions of others as correct?

2. What are the eight weapons of influence?
3. How does this information pertain to you?

Thought Reform and the Psychology of Totalism, Chapter 5 (Lifton, 1961)

1. What does Lifton call the outstanding psychiatric fact of thought reform?
2. What are the eleven psychological steps to death and rebirth Lifton outlines?
3. About what did the released prisoners have profound struggles?
4. How does this information pertain to you?

Thought Reform and the Psychology of Totalism, Chapter 12 (Lifton, 1961)

1. What were the four psychological principles faced when the prisoners returned home?
2. What does each principle mean?
3. What is the fear and relief of total annihilation?
4. What were the beneficial effects of the prisoners' experience?
5. How does this information pertain to you?

Thought Reform and the Psychology of Totalism, Chapter 22 (Lifton, 1961)

Answer the following statements TRUE or FALSE. If a question is FALSE, what is the correct answer?

1. Some potential for extremes exists within everyone. (T/F)
2. Loaded Language is the most basic feature of thought reform. (T/F)
3. Milieu Control seeks to establish control over the individual's communication with the outside world and with himself. (T/F)
4. The pressure of milieu control causes the individual to close down as he is deprived of external information and inner reflection. (T/F)
5. The mystique of the group makes manipulating others and oneself, no matter how bizarre or painful, mandatory. (T/F)
6. The Demand for Purity allows plenty of room for every expression and idea. (T/F)
7. Ideological totalists are able to use the universal tendencies toward guilt and shame as emotional levers for their controlling and manipulating influence. (T/F)

8. The Cult of Confession is a vehicle for personal purification, an act of symbolic self-surrender and of exposure which makes it almost impossible to attain a reasonable balance between worth and humility. (T/F)

9. To the totalist the Sacred Science is one of several moral visions for the ordering of human existence. (T/F)

10. The clichés of totalist language become the start and finish of any ideological analysis. (T/F)

11. The effect of totalist language is the constriction of human thought and emotion. (T/F)

12. Doctrine Over Person honors the uniqueness of individual experience. (T/F)

13. The doctrine subordinates to (accommodates) human character and experience. (T/F)

14. The 'will to orthodoxy' allows for modification of the doctrine in accordance with one's special nature or potentialities. (T/F)

15. The Dispensing of Existence draws a sharp line between those who have a right to exist and those who do not. (T/F)

16. Totalists do not feel themselves compelled to destroy all possibilities of false existence as a means of furthering the great plan of true existence to which they are committed. (T/F)

17. The totalist environment, even when it does not resort to physical abuse, stimulates in everyone a fear of extinction or annihilation. (T/F)

18. An environment need only express two of these eight psychological themes to resemble ideological totalism. (T/F)

19. Every totalist milieu achieves complete totalism. (T/F)

20. The experience of ideological totalism carries a potential rebound effect of retreating into all-or-nothing emotional patterns. (T/F)

21. The capacity for totalism is most fundamentally a product of human childhood, of the prolonged period of helplessness and dependency through which each of us must pass. (T/F)

22. How does this information pertain to you?

The following are essay questions:

1. What is the source of ideological totalism?
2. Under what conditions does man seek to become this guide?
3. How does this information pertain to you?

Appendix C:
Answer Key to Study Questions

Note that some of these materials were written about young people, when most of the people recruited and having left cults were young. The cults now include all age groups. Much of this material is still applicable and to all ages.

Please remember these questions and answers are simply a learning aid. This is not a test to determine your worth. Become aware of any all-or-nothing reactions you may have to this learning process and adjust such expectations.

"Coming Out of the Cults" (Singer, 1979)

1. They expected to learn from the participants and to relieve some of the participants' distress by offering a setting for mutual support. They wanted to help explain the processes and mechanisms for behavior change.
2. During periods of depression and confusion, when they had a sense that life was meaningless.
3. (1) Depression, (2) loneliness, (3) indecisiveness, (4) slipping into altered states, (5) blurring of mental acuity, (6) uncritical passivity, (7) fear of the cult, (8) the fishbowl effect, (9) the agonies of explaining, (10) guilt, (11) perplexities about altruism, (12) money, (13) elite no more.
4. ?

Youth, Brainwashing and the Extremist Cults, Chapter 8 (Enroth, 1977)

1. A search for identity and a quest for spiritual reality that provides clear-cut answers to their questions.
2. (1) Access to potential converts, (2) solicit interest by the potential convert, (3) initiate intense group pressure and group activity, (4) isolate from prior familiar associations and from any "outside" feedback or input, (5) initiate sensory deprivation (especially food and sleep) and sensory bombardment, (6) alter former attitude toward and conception of the world, (7) resocialization by stripping individual of identity, (8) renunciation and rejection of prior associations and relationships. The past is submerged.
3. ?

"Kids 'n' Cults" (Swope, 1980)

1. Perfection, harmony, simplicity.

2. Given the right set of circumstances, almost any young adult can be recruited into a cult.
3. (1) Idealistic, (2) innocent, (3) inquisitive, (4) independent, (5) identity-seeking, (6) insecure.
4. Three or four need to be present.
5. Vulnerability at the time of recruitment.
6. ?

Influence (Cialdini, 1984)

1. When we are unsure of ourselves, when the situation is unclear or ambiguous, when uncertainty reigns.
2. (1) Contrast principle, (2) rule for reciprocation, (3) rejection-then-retreat, (4) commitment and consistency, (5) social proof, (6) liking, (7) authority-directed deference, (8) scarcity.
3. ?

Thought Reform and the Psychology of Totalism, Chapter 5 (Lifton, 1961)

1. The penetration by the psychological forces of the environment into the inner emotions of the individual.
2. (1) Assault upon identity, (2) establishment of guilt, (3) self-betrayal, (4) breaking point of total conflict and basic fear, (5) leniency and opportunity, (6) compulsion to confess, (7) channelling of guilt, (8) reeducation, (9) progress and harmony, (10) final confession , (11) rebirth.
3. Their identity, ability to trust, and search for wholeness (integrity).
4. ?

Thought Reform and the Psychology of Totalism, Chapter 12 (Lifton, 1961)

1. (1) Mastery and integrity, (2) separation, (3) expatriate's return, (4) renewal of identity.
2. (1) Mastery and integrity – subjects relived their thought reform as a means of coming to terms with it and to overcome guilt and shame. They achieve mastery through restoration of integrity. Lecturing and writing were particularly effective ways of achieving mastery;

   (2) Separation – some were mourning the loss of the very special intimacy of the group and the delight in total exposure and sharing. Each mourned a lost part of himself;

   (3) Expatriate's return – almost all felt themselves emotionally removed from those who had not shared their experiences. Their

return is a confrontation with elements of their identity which have been long denied, repressed, or modified beyond easy recognition;

(4) Renewal of identity – this was the overriding task and could contain much confusion as it was difficult to trust sufficiently any one among many identity elements: who they thought they were, who they used to be, who the reformers said they were, and who they wanted to be. This new relationship [understanding of self] that each had to work out was similar to another rebirth.

3. The fear is the possibility of risking its recurrence through reexposure to total control. The relief is that such a repetition would relieve a troubling sense of guilt.

4. ?

Thought Reform and the Psychology of Totalism, Chapter 22 (Lifton, 1961)

(1) T, (2) F—milieu control, the control of human communication, (3) T, (4) T, (5) T, (6) F—the world is divided into the pure and impure, the absolutely good and absolutely evil, (7) T, (8) T, (9) F—it is the ultimate and only vision, (10) T, (11) T, (12) F—it subordinates human experience to the claims of the doctrine and can replace the realities of individual experience, (13) F—the doctrine, including its mythological elements, is ultimately more valid, true and real than is any aspect of actual human character or human experience, (14) F—new rationalizations are required in order to adhere to the doctrine and people must be modified to reaffirm the myth , (15) T, (16) F—they do feel compelled to destroy all possibilities of false existence, (17) T, (18) F—the more clearly an environment expresses these eight psychological themes, the greater its resemblance to ideological totalism, (19) F—no milieu ever achieves complete totalism and many relatively moderate environments show some signs of it, (20) T, (21) T, (22) ?

Essay questions:

1. The source of ideological totalism lies in the ever-present human quest for the omnipotent guide—for the supernatural force, political party, philosophical idea, great leader, or precise science—that will bring ultimate solidarity to all men and eliminate the terror of death and nothingness.

2. During periods of cultural crisis and rapid historical change.

3. ?

Appendix D:
Information on Nutrition and Stress

The following is general information on the nutritional needs of adults. You should check with your doctor or health care professional to tailor these daily requirements to your specific needs. (Source: American Dairy Council, 1990.)

Daily Nutritional Needs

The ideal daily intake for an average adult is as follows:

- Milk/Dairy Products: 2 servings (3 for pregnant or nursing women). 1 serving = 1 cup (or 1 ounce hard cheese).
- Lean Meat/Fish/Poultry/Eggs: 2 to 6 ounces.
- Vegetables: 3 to 5 servings. 1 serving = 1/2 cup or 1 medium vegetable.
- Fruit: 2 to 4 servings. 1 serving = 1/2 cup or 1 medium fruit.
- Bread, Cereal, Pasta, Rice, Beans: 6 or more servings. 1 serving = 1 slice or 1/2 cup.
- Fats and Oils: Up to 6-8 teaspoons.

These servings supply your basic needs. To maintain your healthy weight, add more vegetables, fruit, bread, and cereals. You may also want to consider an all-purpose, high stress vitamin.

Four-Star Foods

These are foods that, as part of a healthy, lowfat diet, are especially helpful:

1. Fish is low in saturated fat and rich in polyunsaturated oils. Try fish as a main dish at least three times a week. Fatty fish (salmon, sardines) are fine.
2. Beans, such as navy beans, lima beans, kidney beans (as in chili), and lentils are all rich in fibers that help lower blood cholesterol.
3. Oat bran and oatmeal are also rich in special fibers that help lower blood cholesterol.
4. Vegetable oil includes polyunsaturated vegetable oils (safflower, corn, sunflower, soybean) and monounsaturated olive and canola oils.

Side Effects of Change

Ask your health care professional if you have any questions or side effects as your diet changes from what the cult fed you. If trying to change your eating or exercise patterns causes you to get disoriented or start floating, you can:

- Stop and give yourself more time to heal.
- Talk about what you are experiencing with someone you trust. Don't isolate yourself.

It takes time and consistent effort to change. Give yourself time and be gentle with yourself.

General Tips for Good Health

Some general tips for overall good health:

- Keep your weight within the range your doctor recommends for you.
- Avoid excessive alcohol and other chemicals, caffeine, fats, sugars, and smoking.
- Try to get regular exercise every day. Brisk walking and stair climbing count, so try to work them into your daily routine whenever you can. For heart fitness, add 20 minutes of aerobic exercise (biking, swimming, etc.) at least three times a week.
- Reward yourself with little treats for making changes in your diet and sticking to them. Treats may include new clothes, books, magazines, movies, sports equipment, or simply time off for something you usually don't get to do.

Minimizing the Effects of Stress

Common signs of stress and anxiety are nervousness, trembling, dizziness, pounding heart, inability to concentrate, inability to slow down or relax, abnormal eating habits, and troubled breathing. (Source: 1969 Parlay International and US Dept. of Health and Human Services.)

There are many ways to keep the negative effects of different stresses to a minimum, including:

- Take time for yourself to relax each day. Perhaps, go away for the weekend or take some time off.
- Get enough sleep and eat a healthy diet.
- Talk out worries with a trusted friend.
- Exercise regularly after getting your doctor's okay (if necessary).
- Learn to "let go" of things which are outside of your control. Learn to adapt to changes.
- Learn to take action when you can make a difference.

- Avoid excessive alcohol and other chemicals, caffeine, fats, sugars, and smoking.
- Set realistic goals. Be practical.
- Give some time to hobbies or other activities.

Remember, healing takes time. Be gentle with yourself.

Appendix E:
Career Planning Worksheet

In this appendix, I have pulled from my ten years' experience working for medium and large corporations some career planning information that has worked for me. This information is not intended to be a substitute for professional career counseling. Entrepreneurs will find this information helpful but not directly relevant.

This abbreviated outline is designed to be used during Phase Three of recovery. Career planning involves assessing what skills you have now, where you want to go with your talents, and how to get there. Moving ahead in your job often involves acquiring additional skills and improving existing ones.

Take time to think through and write down your thoughts. Where appropriate, try to assign a sequence and time frames to acquiring skills. Also, determine what the measurement will be. A measurement is something that enables you to evaluate how far along you are toward completing your goals.

Assess Your Career Goals

1. Identify your needs and rank them in order of priority, such as:
    a. What do you need to be happy?
    b. What does success mean to you?
    c. Are you the primary or secondary wage earner?
    d. Should you work part-time or full-time?
    e. What are your long-range financial needs, such as:
        i. Health and education
        ii. Travel and vacation(s)
        iii. Housing and transportation
        iv. Retirement
    f. Do you want to volunteer for community activities?
2. Identify your interests — what you like and do not like to do.
3. Identify your abilities — what you can and cannot do well.
4. Identify your personality style — what types of people do you and don't you work well with. What effect do you have on others?
5. Identify whether you want to work for yourself or for a company (government, education, business).

6. If you want to run your own business, identify the skills necessary for success. Which skills do you have now and which ones will you need to develop?

7. If you want to work for a company, identify what kind of company you want to work for. What is its:

    a. Culture—its values and ethics
        i. How does it treat people?
        ii. How does it treat the environment?
        iii. Is it responsive to community needs?

    b. Benefit package
        i. Medical and dental coverage
        ii. Life insurance
        iii. Worker's compensation
        iv. Tuition reimbursement

    c. Size and product
        i. Does it make nuclear weapons or raise flower bulbs?
        ii. Will you be one of thousands or one of twenty?

    d. Management style
        i. Does the manager want to make all the decisions or does she want the employee to participate?
        ii. Does the manager look over your shoulder or trust you to come to her with problems?

Build a Career Plan

Once you know what type of job and company you are looking for and why, complete the following:

1. Assign time frames to your priorities and needs. What can you accomplish in 6 months, 1 year, 3 years, 5 years?

2. What are the measurements you can use to assess your progress?

3. Identify the tasks and additional skills you will need to develop:

    a. Interpersonal—getting along with and utilizing the talents of others
        i. Listening
        ii. Questioning
        iii. Teambuilding
        iv. Negotiating
        v. Collaborating

    b. Functional—what does it take to carry out the job?
        i. Decision-making

      ii.   Running meetings

      iii. Giving presentations

      iv. Followthrough

   c. Technical

      i.   Computer competence

      ii.   Analysis of data

   d. Organizational

      i.   Understand how your department fits into the company-wide organizational structure.

      ii.   Understand the roles and responsibilities of others. This will help you get things done and identify inefficient processes.

      iii. Understand the pressures or needs of your manager, such as budget and policy constraints.

Opportunities for Career Development

Remember, you are building a career. Building takes time.

1. Remember that promotions and opportunities to change jobs take time. Rarely is there an instant fix.

2. You have the responsibility to work with your manager to make it happen for you. Don't expect your manager to "save you." Build a development plan with the support of your manager and see it through.

3. Look for opportunities—stay abreast of what's happening in your industry.

4. Look for opportunities—stay abreast of what's happening in your company.

5. Network with other organizations and people. Build relationships that can help you connect with people who can get things done. Also, build relationships with people who can give you constructive feedback.

6. What are the future forces affecting your job? You don't need mystical revelations to figure this out. You need to learn to evaluate your situation, technological advancements, and the effect of the economy on your company.

7. Diversify your job skill set. The economy is constantly changing. As time allows, expand your skill set to ensure you're employable. Stay open to change.

Additional Readings

Additional books and articles that you may find helpful include:

Andersen, S. M. & Zimbardo, P. G. (1984). On Resisting Social Influence. *Cultic Studies Journal. 1*(2), 196–219.

Andres, R. & Lane, J. R. (Eds.). (1988). *Cults and Consequences: The Definitive Handbook.* CA: The Jewish Federation Council of Los Angeles.

Blass, E. M. (Ed). (1988). *Handbook of Behavioral Neurobiology.* Volume 9, NY: Plenum.

Blood, L. (1984). Shepherding/Discipleship: Theology and Practice of Absolute Obedience. *Cultic Studies Journal. 2*(2), 235–245.

Boulette, T. R. & Andersen, S. (1986). "Mind Control" and the Battering of Women. *Cultic Studies Journal. 3*(1), 25–35.

Bussell, H. (1985). Why Evangelicals are Vulnerable to Cults. *Cultic Studies Journal. 2*(2), 259–266.

Cannetti, E. (1984). *Crowds and Power.* NY: Continuum Publishing Co.

Crawley, K., Paulina, D. & White, R. W. (1990). Reintegration of Exiting Cult Members with their Families: A Brief Intervention Model. *Cultic Studies Journal. 7*(1), 26–40.

De Waal, F. (1984). *Chimpanzee Politics.* Narper Colophon, NY.

Dreman, D. (1979). *Contrarian Investment Strategy.* NY: Random House.

Dubrow-Eichel, S. K. (1989). Deprogramming: A Case Study. *Cultic Studies Journal. 6*(2), 1–117.

Dubrow-Eichel, S. K. & Dubrow-Eichel, L. (1988). Trouble in Paradise: Some Observations on Psychotherapy with New Agers. *Cultic Studies Journal. 5*(2), 177–192.

Durden-Smith, J. & deSimone, D.(1983). *Sex and the Brain.* NY: Warner Books.

Edwards, C. (1979). *Crazy for God.* NJ: Prentice-Hall.

Fellows, R. C. (1987/88). Creating the Illusion of Mind Reading in a Self-Transformation Training. *Cultic Studies Journal. 4*(2)/5(1), 44–58.

Galanti, G. A. (1984). Brainwashing and the Moonies. *Cultic Studies Journal.* 1(1), 27–36.

Goldberg L. & Goldberg, W. (1989). Family Responses to a Young Adult's Cult Membership and Return. *Cultic Studies Journal.* 6(1), 86–100.

Goldberg L. & Goldberg, W. (1988). Psychotherapy with Ex-Cultists: Four Case Studies and Commentary. *Cultic Studies Journal.* 5(2), 193–210.

Golding, W. (1955). *Lord of the Flies.* NY: Capricorn.

Greene, F. (1989). Litigating Child Custody with Religious Cults. *Cultic Studies Journal.* 6(1), 69–75.

Henry & Stephens (Eds). (1977). *Stress, Health, and the Social Environment.* NY: Springer-Verlag.

Hoffer, E. (1966). *The True Believer.* NY: Harper Row.

Huxley, A.A. (1952). *The Devils of Loudun.* NY: Harper Colophon.

Jacobson, L. (1986). My Experience in YWAM: A Personal Account and Critique. *Cultic Studies Journal.* 3(2), 204–233.

Kandell, R. F. (1987/88). Litigating the Cult-Related Child Custody Case. *Cultic Studies Journal.* 4(2)/5(1), 122–131.

Kertzer, D. (1988). *Ritual, Politics, and Power.* CT: New Haven.

Kindleberger, C. P. (1978). *Manias, Panics, and Crashes.* NY: Basic Books.

Konner, M. (1982). *The Tangled Wing.* NY: Harper Colophon.

Lalich, J. (1992). The Cadre Ideal: Origins and Development of a Political Cult. *Cultic Studies Journal.* 9(1), 1–77.

Langone, M. D. (1985). Cult Involvement: Suggestions for Concerned Parents and Professionals. *Cultic Studies Journal.* 2(1), 148–168.

Langone, M. D. (Ed.) (in press). *Recovery from Cults: Help for Victims of Psychological and Spiritual Abuse.* NY: Norton.

LeBar, J. J. (1989). *Cults, Sects, and the New Age.* Huntington, IN: Our Sunday Visitor.

Levy, L. (1990). Prosecuting an Ex-Cult Member's Undue Influence Suit. *Cultic Studies Journal.* 7(1), 15–25.

Liebowitz, M. R. (1983). *The Chemistry of Love.* NY: Berkley Books.

Lifton, R. J. (1991). Cult Formation. *Cultic Studies Journal.* 8(1), 1–6.

Litfin, A. D. (1985). The Perils of Persuasive Preaching. *Cultic Studies Journal.* 2(2), 267–273.

MacDonald, G. (1985). Disciple Abuse. *Cultic Studies Journal.* 2(2), 288–295.

Malcolm, A. (1975). *The Tyranny of the Group.* Totowa, NY: Littlefield, Adams and Co.

Markowitz, A. & Halperin, D. (1984). Cults and Children: The Abuse of the Young. *Cultic Studies Journal.* 1(2), 143–155.

McDonald, J. P. (1987/88). "Reject the Wicked Man"--Coercive Persuasion and Deviance Production: A Study of Conflict Management. *Cultic Studies Journal.* 4(2)/5(1), 59–121.

Meerloo, J. A. (1961). *Rape of the Mind.* NY: Grosset and Dunlap.

Milgram, S. (1975). *Obedience to Authority.* NY: Harper.

Miller, J. S. (1986). The Utilization of Hypnotic Techniques in Religious Conversion. *Cultic Studies Journal.* 3(2), 243–250.

Ofshe, R. & Singer, M. T. (1986). Attacks on Peripheral versus Central Elements of Self and the Impact of Thought Reforming Techniques. *Cultic Studies Journal.* 3(1), 3–24.

Patrick, T. & Dulack, T. (1976). *Let Our Children Go.* NY: Ballantine Books.

Randi, J. (1986). *Flim Flam! Psychics, ESP, Unicorns and Other Delusions.* Buffalo, NY: Prometheus Books.

Reimers, A. J. (1986). Charismatic Covenant Community: A Failed Promise. *Cultic Studies Journal.* 3(1), 36–56.

Reite, M. & Field, T. (Eds). (1985). *The Psychobiology of Attachment and Separation.* Orlando, FL: Academic Press.

Ross, J. & Langone, M. (1988). *Cults: What Parents Should Know.* Weston, MA: American Family Foundation.

Rudin, M. (1984). *Cults on Campus: Continuing Challenge.* Weston, MA: American Family Foundation.

Rudin, J. & Rudin, M. (1980). *Prison or Paradise? The New Religious Cults.* Philadelphia, PA: Fortress Press.

Sargant, W. (1957). *Battle for the Mind.* NY: Doubleday and Co., Inc.

Scharff, G. (1985). Autobiography of a Former Moonie. *Cultic Studies Journal.* 2(2), 252–258.

Singer, M. T., Temerlin, M. & Langone, M. D. (1990). Psychotherapy Cults. *Cultic Studies Journal.* 7(2), 101–125.

Sowell, T. (1987). *A Conflict of Visions.* NY: Morrow.

Stoner, C. (1977). *All Gods Children.* Radnor, PA: Chilton.

Temerlin, J. W. & Temerlin, M. K. (1986). Some Hazards of the Therapeutic Relationship. *Cultic Studies Journal.* 3(2), 234–242.

Tobias, M. & Lalich, J. (in press). *Captive Hearts, Captive Minds.* Alameda, CA: Hunter House.

West, L. J. (1990). Persuasive Techniques in Contemporary Cults: A Public Health Approach. *Cultic Studies Journal.* 7(2), 126–149.

References/Bibliography

A Comeback for Religious Cults? (1980, November 24). *U.S. News and World Report*.

Al-Anon's Twelve Steps and Twelve Traditions. (1986). NY: Al-Anon Family Group Headquarters Inc.

Andersen, Susan M. and Zimbardo, Philip G. (1984). On Resisting Social Influence. *Cultic Studies Journal. 1*(2), 196–219.

Andron, S. (Speaker). (1987). *Preventive Education* (Cassette recording, 1987 CAN/AFF Regional Conference, Sturbridge, MA). Chicago, IL: Cult Awareness Network.

Auel, J. M. (1980). *The Clan of the Cave Bear.* MA: Bantam Books.

Auel, J. M. (1982). *The Valley of Horses.* MA: Bantam Books.

Bachelder, L. (1966). *The Understanding Heart.* Mt. Vernon, NY: The Peter Pauper Press.

Barauch, G., Barnett, R. & Rivers, C. (1984, May). Today's Baby Boomers. *Ladies' Home Journal.*

Bar-Yam Hassan, A. & Bar-Yam, M. (1987). Interpersonal Development Across the Life Span: Communion and Its Interaction with Agency in Psychosocial Development. *Contributions to Human Development, 18,* 102–128.

Behrens, D. (1982, August). The Cult Crisis. *Glamour.*

Black, C. (1982). *It Will Never Happen to Me!* Denver, CO: M.A.C..

Blakeslee, S. (1990, March). New Connections. *American Health.*

Blueprint for Progress: Al-Anon's Fourth-Step Inventory. (1976). NY: Al–Anon Family Group Headquarters.

Bly, R. (1990). *Iron John.* MA: Addison–Wesley Publishing Co., Inc.

Bolles, R. N. (1971). *What Color is Your Parachute?* Berkley, CA: Ten Speed Press.

Branden, N. (1971). *The Disowned Self.* NY: Bantam Books.

Breucher, F. (1991). *Telling Secrets.* NY: HarperCollins Publishers.

Bridges, W. (1980). *Transitions.* MA: Addison-Wesley Publishing Co., Inc.

Bucke, R. M. (1923). *Cosmic Consciousness.* NY: E.P. Dutton and Co., Inc.

Bussell, H. L. (1983). *Unholy Devotion, Why Cults Lure Christians.* Grand Rapids, MI: Zondervan Publishing House.

Bussell, H. (1981, June). Why Evangelicals are Vulnerable to Cults. *The Gordon, 26*(2), June 1981.

Carnegie, D. (1936). *How to Win Friends and Influence People.* NY: Simon and Schuster.

Channeling. (1987, February 9). [TV Program]. Channel 5. San Francisco, CA.

Channeling. (1987, February 15). [TV Program]. Town Meeting.

Cialdini, R. B. (1984). *Influence, the New Psychology of Modern Persuasion.* NY: William Morrow and Co., Inc.

Clark, J.G., Langone, M.D., Schecter, R.E. & Daley, R.C.B. (1981). *Destructive Cult Conversion: Theory, Research, and Treatment.* Weston, MA: American Family Foundation.

Clark, J.G. (1979, July 20). Cults. *Journal of the American Medical Association, 242*(3), 279–281.

Clougherty, J. (1992). *The Boston Church of Christ: Church or Cult?* Unpublished undergraduate paper, Harvard University, Cambridge, MA.

Conway, F. & Siegelman, J. (1978). *Snapping, America's Epidemic of Sudden Personality Change.* NY: Lippincott Co.

Cults. (1988, November). [TV Program]. 48 Hours. New York, NY.

Cults and Media. (1990). (Cassette recording, 1990 CAN Conference, PA). Chicago, IL: Cult Awareness Network.

Cummins, H. J. (1980, August 10). Cult or Calling. *Democrat and Chronicle.*

Deal, T. E. & Kennedy, A. (1982). *Corporate Cultures.* MA: Addison-Wesley Publishing Co., Inc.

Delgado, R. (1978, December 27). Investigating Cults. *The New York Times.*

Dellinger, R. W. (1985). *Cults and Kids, A Study of Coercion.* Boystown, Nebraska: The Boys Town Center.

Denton, A. A. (1978, May 31). Uproar in Emporia. *The Christian Century*.

Diamant, A. (1988, August). The Big Lie. *Boston Magazine*.

Diamant, A. (1987, November). The Complaints of a New Generation. *Boston Magazine*.

Diamant, A. (1986, July 20). Mind Matters. *The Boston Globe Magazine*.

DiGiovanni, N. & Lane, E. (1979, June). God's Puppets. *Westchester Illustrated*.

Dreifus, (1987, July 5). C. We're Tougher Than We Think. *Parade Magazine*, p. 10.

Dujardin, R. C. (1980, August 2). The Way: A Commando Course for Armageddon? *The Providence Journal-Bulletin*.

Enroth, R. (1980, Spring). The Supposed Gulf Between True Belief and False. *United Evangelical Action*.

Enroth, R. (1977). *Youth, Brainwashing and the Extremist Cults*. Grand Rapids, MI: Zondervan Publishing House.

Ex-Member Panel. (1987). (Cassette recording, 1987 CAN/AFF Regional Conference, Sturbridge, MA). Chicago, IL: Cult Awareness Network.

Fisher, R. & Ury, W. (1981). *Getting to Yes*. NY: Penguin Books.

Fox, M. F. & Hesse-Biber, S. (1984). *Women at Work*. NY: Mayfield Publishing Co.

Freed, J. (1980). *Moonwebs, Journey into the Mind of a Cult*. Toronto, Ontario: Dorset Publishing, Inc.

Friedan, B. (1963). *The Feminine Mystique*. NY: Norton.

Friedrich, O. (1987, December 7). New Age Harmonies. *Time Magazine*.

Galanter, M. (1982, December 10). Charismatic Religious Sects and Psychiatry: An Overview. *American Journal of Psychiatry*, 139(12), 1539–1548.

Gallagher, K. A. *(1978). Cultism and Free Thought*. Unpublished paper.

Geraldo. (1988, November). [TV Program]. New York, NY.

Giambalvo, C. (1991). *Exit Counseling: A Family Intervention*. Weston, MA: American Family Foundation.

Giambalvo, C. (1988). *Multiplying Ministries (Crossroads) Compared to Lifton's Criteria for Thought Reform.* Unpublished paper.

Gilligan, C. (1982). *In A Different Voice.* Cambridge, MA: Harvard University Press.

Gladstone, B. (1980). Should We Shackle the Cults? *Quest.*

Goldberg, W. & Goldberg, L. (Speakers). (1987). *FOCUS-Understanding Parents' Experience* (Cassette recording, 1987 CAN/AFF Regional Conference, Sturbridge, MA). Chicago, IL: Cult Awareness Network.

Gustaitis, R. (1980). Hard-Sell Religion. *Nutshell.*

Harden, M. (1979, July). The Way. *Ohio Magazine.*

Harris, R. (1976). *Freedom Spent.* Boston, MA: Little, Brown and Company.

The Harvard Nuclear Study Group. (1983). *Living with Nuclear Weapons.* NY: Bantam Books.

Hassan, S. (1988). *Combatting Cult Mind Control.* VT: Park Street Press.

Heilbroner, R. L. (1980). *The Worldly Philosophers.* NY: Simon and Schuster.

Heller, R. K. (1982). *Deprogramming for Do-It-Yourselfers: A Cure for the Common Cult.* Medina, OH: The Gentle Press.

Heller, R. K. (1980). *An Opinion: The Relevance of Hypnosis to Acculturation.* Unpublished paper.

Herman, J. L. (1992). *Trauma and Recovery.* US: Basic Books.

Hochman, J. (Ed.) (1990, April). Cults [special issue]. *Psychiatric Annals. 20*(4).

Howard, V. A. & Barton, J. H. (1986). *Thinking on Paper.* NY: William Morrow and Co., Inc.

Humphry, D. (1991). *Final Exit.* Eugene, OR: The Hemlock Society.

Hypnotized for Tests She Turned Killer for CIA. (1978, February 21). *The Detroit Free Press.*

Kraft, J. R. (1988). *Understanding Cults.* Unpublished undergraduate paper, Harvard University, Cambridge, MA.

Kübler-Ross, E. (1969). *On Death and Dying.* NY: Macmillian Publishing Co.

Langone, M. (1988). *Cults: Questions and Answers.* Weston, MA: American Family Foundation.

Langone, M. (1982). *Destructive Cultism: Questions and Answers.* Weston, MA: American Family Foundation.

Lerner, R. (1985, January/February). Co-Dependency: The Swirl of Energy Surrounded by Confusion. *Focus on Family.*

Levine, A. (1986, February). The Great Subliminal Self-Help Hoax. *New Age Journal.*

Levine, S. V. (1984, August). Communal Groups. *Psychology Today.*

Lifton, R. J. (1961). *Thought Reform and the Psychology of Totalism.* NY: W.W. Norton and Co., Inc.

Lifton, R. J. & Singer, M. T. (Speakers). (1989). *Untitled.* (Cassette recording, 1989 CAN Conference, NY). Chicago, IL: Cult Awareness Network.

Lifton, R. J. (Speaker). (1989). *Untitled.* (Cassette recording, 1989 CAN Conference, NY). Chicago, IL: Cult Awareness Network.

MacCollam, J. A. (1977, November). The Way' Seemed Right but the End Thereof. *Eternity.*

Mackay, C. (1980). *Extraordinary Popular Delusions and the Madness of Crowds.* NY: Harmony Books.

Maslow, A. H. *Some Basic Propositions of Holistic-Dynamic Psychology.* Unpublished paper, Brandeis University, Boston, MA.

Masters, R. D. (1989). *The Nature of Politics.* New Haven, CT: Yale.

McKelvey, V. (1979). Way's Assets Draw Criticism. *Journal Herald.*

McFarland, B. & Baker-Baumann, T. (1988). *Feeding the Empty Heart.* NY: Harper and Row, Publishers, Inc.

National Association of Secondary School Principals & International Cult Education Program. (1987). *Cults: Saying 'No' Under Pressure* [Videotape]. Weston, MA: American Family Foundation.

Newman, M. & Berkowitz, B. (1971). *How to Be Your Own Best Friend.* NY: Random House, Inc.

New Religious Groups: Membership and Legal Battles. (1979, January). *Psychology Today*.

Nicholi, A. M. (1974, April). A New Dimension of the Youth Culture. *American Jouranl of Psychiatry, 131*(4).

Ornstein, R. & Thompson, R. F. (1984). *The Amazing Brain*. Boston, MA: Houghton Mifflin Company.

Orwell, G. (1954). *Nineteen Eighty-Four.* Middlesex, England: Penguin.

Peck, M. S. (1978). *The Road Less Traveled.* NY: Simon and Schuster.

People Are Talking. (1988, November). [TV Program]. Boston, MA.

Prather, H. (1977). *Notes on Love and Courage.* NY: Doubleday and Co., Inc.

Psychics. (1987, February 22). [TV Program]. Town Meeting.

Ramniceanu, N. (1979, September 20). A Ride in a Green Mercedes: My Summer Vacation. *Amherst Student*.

Ray, J. L. (1983). *Global Politics*. Boston, MA: Houghton Mifflin Company.

Reiter, M. (1981, October). One Man's Story. *50 Plus*.

Religious Cult Investigated. (1981, April 14). *The Boston Globe*.

Rockmore, M. (1980, October). Hypnosis: A Drug Substitute? *American Way*.

Ross, J. C. & Langone, M. (1988). *Cults, What Parents Should Know.* Weston, MA: American Family Foundation.

Rubin, L. B. (1983). *Intimate Strangers.* NY: Harper and Row, Publishers.

Ruddick, S. & Daniels, P. (1977). *Working It Out.* NY: Pantheon Books.

Rudin, M. (1981, October). New Target of the Cults: You. *50 Plus*.

Schecter, R. E. & Noyes, W. L. (Eds.). (1987). *Cultism on Campus.* Weston, MA: American Family Foundation and the National Association of Student Personnel Administrators, Inc.

Sheehy, G. (1976). *Passages.* NY: E.P. Dutton and Co., Inc.

Short and Long Term After Effects of Cult Involvement. (1987). (Cassette recording, 1987 CAN/AFF Regional Conference, Sturbridge, MA). Chicago, IL: Cult Awareness Network.

Singer, M. T. (1979, January). Coming Out of the Cults. *Psychology Today, 72–81.*

Smith, Z. N. (1981, April 12). Cult Tie at Tank Plant Probed. *Chicago Sun Times.*

Some Home Truths About The Way International. (1980, August). *Searchlight.*

Sparks, J. N. (1977). *The Mind Benders.* NY: Thomas Nelson Publishers.

Spero, J. E. (1985). *The Politics of International Economic Relations.* NY: St. Martin's Press.

Stoner, C. & Kisser, C. (1992). *Touchstones, Reconnecting After a Cult Experience.* Chicago, IL: Cult Awareness Network, 1992.

Swope, G. W. (1980, May/June). Kids 'n' Cults. *Media and Methods.* PA: North American Publishing Company.

Tannen, D. (1990). *You Just Don't Understand.* NY: Ballantine Books.

Terris, D. (1986, June 8). Come, All Ye Faithful. *The Boston Globe Magazine.*

Terzani, T. (1980, October 21). A Touch of 1984. *The Boston Globe.*

Trepman, E. (1988, Spring). The Oath Betrayed, The Physician Soldiers of Nazi Germany. *Harvard Medical.*

You Can Go Home Again. [Videotape]. Los Angeles, CA: Jewish Federation Film.

Vaughan, C. (1982). *Addictive Drinking.* NY: Penguin Books.

The Wave. [Film].

Wallis, C. (1989, December 4). Onward, Women! *Time Magazine.*

Wein, B. (1987, April). Body and Soul Music. *American Health.*

West, L. J. (Speaker). (1987). *Psychiatric Reflections on Cults* (Cassette recording, 1987 CAN/AFF Regional Conference, Sturbridge, MA). Chicago, IL: Cult Awareness Network.

West, L. J. (Speaker). (1987). *Special Address* (Cassette recording, 1987 CAN/AFF Regional Conference, Sturbridge, MA). Chicago, IL: Cult Awareness Network.

Whitfield, C. L. (1987). *Healing the Child Within.* Deerfield Beach, FL: Health Communications.

Williams, R. C. & Cantelon, P. L. (1984). *The American Atom.* Philadelphia, PA: Un. of Pennsylvania Press.

Woititz, J. G. (1983). *Adult Children of Alcoholics.* Pompano Beach, FL: Health Communications, Inc.

Woititz, J. G. (1983). *Struggle for Intimacy.* Pompano Beach, FL: Health Communications, Inc.